The Life and Times of
WARREN BUFFETT

The Life and Times of
WARREN BUFFETT

Dinkar Kumar

Ocean Books Pvt. Ltd.
ISO 9001:2008 Publishers

Published by
Ocean Books (P) Ltd.
4/19 Asaf Ali Road,
New Delhi-110 002 (INDIA)
e-mail: info@oceanbooks.in

ISBN 978-81-8430-377-3
The Life and Times of
WARREN BUFFETT
by Dinkar Kumar

Translated by
Dr. R.P. Jain

Edition
2018

Price
₹ 400.00 (Rupees Four Hundred only)

Printed at
S.B.M. Industries Pvt. Ltd., Rai (Har.)

Author's Note

The world hardly knows him by Warren Buffett than, the magician of the share market', 'Omaha's Saint', the Emperor of Berkshire, 'the biggest player of Wall Street and the Oracle of Omaha'. A person with normal strature and jolly nature, nobody can guess that he is the world's third richest and Americas' second richest person. In the issue of April 2007 of Forbes magazine, he got the third place in the list of the world's billionaires, after Bill Gates of America and Carlos Slim Helu of Mexico. He created history in the field of Philanthropy by donating 37 billion dollars (83 per cent of his total wealth) to the Bill and Melindia Gates Foundation (31 billion) not only this, he donated 6 billion for other four charitable trusts for the welfare of world's need.

The story of young Warren Buffett's struggle is like a case study for the students studying management worldwide. The story of Warren Buffett, who sold chewing gums, soda, coke and newspaper to school children in America is narrated often to inculcate the value of self-dependence.

To understand Warren Buffett's personality or to form an opinion about him is as complex as understanding the share market. On one hand, he keeps track of stock and shares in the Wall Street, on the other hand he does not hesitate to donate most of his wealth in charity.

This book tries to explain this complexity by looking into different aspects of his life which are filled with qualities like struggle, restraint, frugality, philanthropy and foresight.

Contents

1

Earning and Spending Skills

American Warren Buffett's name does not need any introduction. There is no business magazine, newspaper or TV channel in the world which does not cover or discusses him. After Bill Gates and Carlos Slim, he is the third richest person in the world. There are several reasons why he is counted in the world's richest's list. Here, we are not discussing him for being rich rather we are here to highlight the fact of his lifestyle, which he embraced in spite of possessing huge amount of wealth.

In our country, every now and then, we witness the arrogant display of pomp and show of the novo rich. But Warren is totally unlike the other rich persons of the world in all respects. Warren, who has a sharp eye over his business, possesses several qualities which distinguish him from the others.

There is no account of the wealth which he possesses, but in America he is the second richest person after Bill Gates. According to 'Forbes Magazine', he is worth 65.1 billion dollars (4297 billion Indian rupees). He created history by donating 83 per cent of his wealth in charity. Warren still lives in the house which he purchased in 1953.

Now let us also find out how he earned the immense wealth and what he does with it.

Warren was born in Nebraska, Omaha on 30th August, 1930. His father was a stock broker. At the age of eleven Warren joined his father's stock broking business and also sold newspapers to earn his pocket money. At the age of thirteen, he filed his first income tax return. He regretted the fact that he started his money earning career pretty late. At the age of fifteen, Warren along with his school classmate set up a pinball machine in a barber's shop by investing 25 dollars. He made good money and bought a 40 acre farm.

He then used his business acumen and started investing in the share market and made lots of money.

At the age of twenty after being unable to get admission in America's reputed Harvard Business School, Warren sought admission in the Columbia Business School. There he learned the tricks of investing in the share market from economic Gurus like Benjamin Graham and David Dodd.

Warren has been known as the Oracle of Omaha or 'Omaha's Saint.' Warren is the single largest investor in several large American companies, of which Coca Cola, Gillette etc. That is to say that irrespective of whosoever might be the promoter or may be running these companies, the real owner is Warren.

Warren's simple lifestyle contrasts with his immense wealth. Warren still lives in the house which he bought fifty eight years earlier. He drives his own car. He neither employs a driver or a security guard. He never travels in a private plane. His company Berkshire Hathway owns 63 companies. He only writes one letter every year to all his CEOs in which he give details of the plans for a complete year.

He never conduct meetings with his Officers or his business associates. He has specified two rules for all his

Officers – one, never allow your shareholders wealth to erode in any manner and second, never forget rule one. He never attends parties of important and influential people.

His message to the youth of the new generation:

"Stay away from the mentality of using the credit card compulsorily and invest on yourself. Wealth has not created mankind but mankind has created wealth. Live your life in the simplest manner possible."

□

2

Story of the World's Most Successful Investor

The nineteenth century was coming to an end. With the rise of Europe, America was emerging as a super power. After the social and industrial upheaval, the lives of people were gradually becoming normal. The conditions in Nebraska District situated on the banks of Missouri river in America were more or less similar. Due to the efforts of its hard working farmers Omaha, a big city of the famous Nebraska was getting back on its feet. But for the Buffett family, living there, the days of struggle were far from over.

In the year 1869 Warren's grandfather opened a small grocery store to earn his living. Grandfather Buffett's business acumen coupled with his good behaviour resulted in the grocery store doing well in a very short time. Gradually the store became his hallmark. His family of two sons started growing.

Warren's father Howard Homan was studying in Nebraska University. Here he met Leila Stahl. While working together for the universities newspaper 'Daily Nebraska', their closeness led to marriage. On 30th August, 1930 in Omaha, a son was born in their house. He was their second child after their daughter Doris and was named Warren Edward Buffett. Warren meant, 'keeper' and he justified his name in the future.

Even though they continued to struggle, the Buffett family was always on the lookout for new rightful business opportunities. Warren's father Howard's interest was less in his father's store and more in the stock market and politics. Seeing his family's hardship, nobody could understand as to when Warren learnt the alphabet of self-sufficiency. To improve the financial condition of his family little Warren also started earning. Little Warren unlike other children of his age, who would be playing and having fun after school, would be involved in earning quarters, dimes and nickels.

Profit from Selling Chewing Gum and Some Innocent Questions

His father's business was still shaky and his grandfather was somehow managing the family through his grocery store. Warren would observe all this, think about it and ask his grandfather as to why their condition was like that? Why are we struggling so much? Can't we become rich quickly? His grandfather would evade his queries and assign him odd jobs. Reminiscing about his childhood on CNBC TV Warren said, "I must have been 7-8 years old, my grandfather would sell chewing gum to me from the store; I would go door-to-door, sell it and earn a few nickels profit. He would sell 6 bottles of coke to me for a quarter and I would sell them and earn a nickel profit. Doing such small odd jobs and earning a small profit became my favourite past time. I was always on the lookout for doing something new and earning a little more profit."

In addition to selling chewing gum, soda and coke, Warren started making schemes along with his schoolmates to earn profit. He worked out a mathematical formula and named it 'Stable Boy Selection', to find out the probable winner in horse racing. He would sell tips to find out the winning horse for a few dollars outside the race course. But before he could earn much, he had to stop it, as he did not have a license for this job. After all why was a 4 feet tall, 10 year old boy so serious about earning money, when he could have enjoyed a carefree life!

But Warren was not at all interested in having fun, all he wanted to do was to earn profit, his habit had turned into an obsession. But the good thing was that whatever he did, he did it honestly and seriously. Cheating did not suit him. When he could not think of doing anything new, he would go and help his grandfather at the store. He would also learn the tricks of the trade.

At 13, A Stock Market Player

During 1941, when the world was embroiled in the Second World War, Warren was also preparing for his own war. He started getting involved in his father's stock broking business. Even though his father could not spare any time to explain the intricacies of the stock market, Warren started understanding the rise and fall of the stock markets on his own. He was able to understand that 'bull' and 'bear' were not animals but were terminology used to describe a rising and falling market, respectively.

Eventually at the age of eleven, he made his first investment in the stock market. He bought 3 shares of Cities Service Preferred at 38 dollars per share. He bought 2 shares in his name and 1 share in his sister Doris's name. But his luck did not favour him, the market entered a bear phase and the shares of Cities Service dropped to 27 dollars a share. But Warren was not discouraged and he held on to the shares till they rose to 40 dollars a share and then he sold them. He regretted for his decision later as the shares of Cities Service rose to 200 dollars a share. This event taught him his first and basic rule that one must exercise control; investment in the shares should be for long durations. This rule helped him to become the most successful investor in the world. At this tender age, Warren who had a completely different identity when compared to his classmates. He had clearly realised two things about himself–one, that he can be successful and second, he can earn money from the work in which he had interest. He was saving money and building his courage to implement both these self-realisations. The only thing that was diminishing was his fear and hesitation.

He was able to strike a balance between studying his school books and using his business acumen. To protect himself and to do something different, he was encouraged by his father to file his income tax return. At that time, Warren was only 13 yrs old. He claimed rebate on expense on his cycle as 'being an expense for conducting his business, when he filled in the details of income and expense for income tax return.

New Location, New Business, Studies and Family

In 1942, the Buffett family moved from Omaha to Washington D.C. so that his father could fulfil his political ambitions. The struggle to re-establish in a new place started all over again. On arriving in Washington, his father became involved in his work, Warren also increased his activities. He became a paper delivery boy. He distributed papers in the streets of Washington and its posh colonies, in morning and evening. He carried two papers with him, 'The Washington Post' and 'The Times Harold', so that if anyone stopped one paper, he could offer the second paper and continue maintaining his clientele. Gradually, he increased the number of papers to five and started selling different magazines also.

He was able to earn about 175 dollars a month, which was equivalent to a grown up man's earning. He was able to save nearly 1200 dollars in a few months. He took a bold step and bought 40 acres of farmland in Thurston County and hired it out to a farmer. It was interesting to note that nobody in the Buffett family could achieve what Warren achieved at the age of 14. Now he was no longer an ordinary boy, he was a land owner.

As Warren was growing older, his understanding was becoming sharper and clearer. Like his classmates, he was not interested in picnics, parties, football, rugby or having girl friends. He distanced himself from all such activities and was busy in creating a new world for himself. At the age of 15, along with one of his classmates, formed a company called, 'Venture Wilson Line Updated Machine Corp', to set up pinball machines. They would place pinball machines in barber's shops and earn up to 50 dollars a week.

It was not as if his family was not aware of his activities. Even though he had got full freedom from his family, yet along with his father, his family desired that he should study properly and do something big. Seeing that his involvement in small and transient jobs was affecting his studies, his father Howard insisted on sending him to University of Pennsylvania's famous, 'Wharton Business School.' Warren was not at all interested in going there. At that time he had 50,000 dollars and he was dreaming to multiply it several times by investing in new businesses. But he had to give up to his father's pressure and he joined Wharton. Though he was not very happy to go to Wharton but anyhow he completed two years of study there and returned home. He completed his last year of study at University of Nebraska in Lincoln. When he reached Nebraska, he returned to his old form. He tied up with the University's paper, 'Lincoln Journal' and took up the responsibility of managing a team of 50 boys for its distribution in six rural districts.

After completing his one year study in Nebraska, he applied for doing post graduation in the reputed Harvard Business School. But the School rejected his application on the grounds that he was underage and will have to wait for two years. However, he was able to get admission in

Columbia Business School. Here he completed his M.S. under the guidance of the famous market analyst Benjamin Graham. His association with Graham paved his way to new heights, which he was very anxious to attain.

Association with Graham, Marriage with Susan

The year was 1949 and Warren was 19 years old. While in Columbia for his Master's degree, Warren got an opportunity to read Benjamin Graham's famous book, 'The Intelligent Investor.' After reading the book he realised that he had not made any mistake in joining Columbia Business School. His understanding of proper and steady investment planning matured. In two years, under the guidance of other Investment Guru's (apart from Graham) like Phillip Fisher, David Dodd, Walter, Walter Schloss and Edwin Kahan, Warren himself became a Guru. Benjamin Graham considered Warren as his best student and placed him in the A+ category.

In 1951, Warren completed his Masters Degree in Economics from Columbia and started formulating his future plans. Warren wanted to work in association with Graham, but Graham refused. Warren had now turned into an intelligent and capable young man and he saw no valid reason to stay at Columbia. Planning to use his academic knowledge in his father's brokerage firm, he returned to Washington and started working as an investment salesman. It was not as if he had given up his desire to work with Graham. He still wished for a chance to work with Graham, so he continued to pursue Graham. Finally he received an offer from Graham to work for him at an annual salary of 12,000 dollars. Warren worked with Graham for two years and gained practical and professional knowledge of all the tricks of the trade which he had studied in Columbia.

During this period he met Susan Thompson. She was a singer in a night club. Their meetings turned into love and led to marriage.

In 1954, when Graham decided to retire and close down his business, Warren and Graham separated. Warren returned to Omaha, but this time he had with him Susan and the tricks of the trade taught by Graham. He now had an open field to trade in the stock market and to do whatever he wished.

From Buffett Associates to Berkshire Hathaway

In 1956, Warren formed a partnership firm 'Buffett Associates.' In this firm, apart from Warren, there were 8 other partners, consisting of his family members and friends. Warren invested 105,000 dollars and the other 8 partners totally invested an equal amount, that is, 105,000 dollars. This partnership firm operated very successfully for nearly 13 years and established Warren's identity in Wall Street. The partnership firm's investment grew by 30 per cent annually, whereas the market grew by 7 to 11 per cent annually. The tricks of the trade which he had leant from Graham played an important role in this achievement.

As his investment grew, his courage also reached new heights and he thought of doing something new. In 1962, Warren started buying shares of a struggling textile company called, 'Berkshire Hathaway.' The immediate Vice-President of Hathaway called it Warren's mistake, as during that period, all the textile companies were incurring losses. However, that did not deter Warren. He increased his holding to 49 per cent at less than 8 dollars a share. He now focused all his attention to turning the biggest deal of his life, so far, to a profitable one.

He also started investing the available funds into acquisitions in public limited companies. Strategically, on the top of his hit list were insurance companies. He got a positive response from the market on account of his good track record. By now, Charlie Munger had become his trusted associate. After Benjamin Graham, Charlie Munger had impressed him the most. Now his investment strategy was armed with the experience of Charlie Munger, in addition to the fundamentals of Graham.

Gradually, Warren effectuated a successful turnaround of the company and brought Berkshire out of loss. It had now become his leading company. To strengthen it further, he merged all his other partnership firms into Berkshire and made his partners shareholders of it. Warren had estimated that the Dow Jones Industrial Index's growth would be about 10 per cent every year. Between the years 1957 and 1969, if someone had invested 10,000 dollars then it would have become 28,570 dollars in 1969, whereas if someone had invested in Buffett's firm then it would have become 150,350 dollars, that too after deducting Warren's share. These figures indicate Warren's business acumen and his involvement.

In the 70's decade, it was being said that if Warren showed interest in any company, then the shares of that company would rise by 10 per cent overnight. In case of some companies, it did actually happen. From 1962 to 1980, the shares of Berkshire rose from 8 dollars to 800 dollars and in 1990 it rose to over 7,000 dollars. He limited his salary to 50,000 dollars annually initially and later raised it 100,000 dollars annually. He maintained a strict control over his expenses. Replying to a colleague he said that whatever he gets by the way of income, he invests a large portion of it in Berkshire and retains the rest for his expenses.

After the turnaround of the business, Warren sold the yarn mill of Berkshire and converted it to a purely holding company, which had investments companies which were growing at a healthy rate. Some of these companies were Washington Post, Coca Cola, Gillette, and American Express, in which Warren started acquiring core holdings, that too for long periods. He also continued to acquire smaller companies. The share price of Berkshire kept on rising and so did the wealth of Warren. He kept on rising to new heights and entered the league of world's richest persons. His wealth can be a source of envy for a lot of business and other tycoons.

Born in the 20th century, he was known as the, 'Saint of Omaha', whereas in the 21st century he was known as the 'Greatest Philanthropist.' In June 2006, he unexpectedly announced donation of 83 per cent of his wealth to the Bill and Melinda Gates Foundation and surprised the world. The contribution amounted to 37 billion dollars or 2400 billion Rupees, which is the largest donation given by anyone in the world. There was a time when he was mocked as the C.E.O., who did not own a private plane. He then bought a private jet for 100 million dollars and silenced all the mockery cast on his extreme austerity.

His decision therefore, to donate a major portion of his vast wealth for philanthropy was indeed a great surprise for the world.

□

3

Wife, Children and Profession

While he was reaching new heights in his profession, he was not happy at home. There was no happiness in his married life and there were signs of cracks. The Warren family consisting of his wife and 3 children were unsatisfied, as he was unable to fulfil his responsibilities towards them. The children were growing up but Warren was not devoting enough time to them. He was completely engrossed in his business. Consequently in 1977 his wife Susan left him and started living in San Francisco. But they stayed in contact.

A waitress named Astrid Menks used to like Warren. After Susan left, she tried to fill the vacuum in Warren's life. The interesting fact is that Astrid was introduced to Warren by Susan herself. In spite of the separation Warren and Susan remained in close contact. They would talk over the phone almost daily, would spend the holidays together and along with the children celebrate Christmas together at their beach house in California. Susan was not disturbed by Astrid's presence. Till Susan died in 2004 due to heart attack, all the three had cordial relations. Two years later on his 75th birthday, Warren formally married Astrid. The arrangements for their marriage were done by his daughter.

Warren's children did not join his business. They chose radically different professions. It could also be on account of Warren's decision to donate his entire wealth for charity. His one son is a photographer and the other son a music composer. His daughter is married; in addition to looking after her family, she is managing Susan Thompson Buffett Foundation and doing charitable work. At the age of 83 Warren and his holding company Berkshire are healthy and active in the world of investing.

While investing money or spending money, Warren is extremely disciplined. In spite of the fact he is a major and an experienced investor in the share market, he does not look for small or quick gains. He had not sold even a single share of his holding in Berkshire. He has been giving his children 10,000 dollars only once in a year on Christmas and that too for claiming rebate on tax. Whenever he helps his children, he does so with proper documentation. Once when his daughter asked him for 20 dollars for parking fee, he paid her by cheque.

Warren prefers to stay in his house in Dundee-Happy Hollow, Omaha which he bought in 1958, 57 years back for 31,500 dollars. In spite of being such a well-known celebrity, he is a very simple person and the people of Omaha do not crowd him. He does not like having bodyguards around him.

□

4

Childhood

In 1942 Warren's father was elected as the Representative to the U.S. House of Representatives from Omaha in Nebraska, for the first time. When the Buffett family moved to Fredericksburg, Virginia (about 50 miles from Washington D.C.), in January, then Warren was allowed to stay in Omaha along with his grandfather and Aunt to complete his 8th class studies. Thereafter, he completed his 9th class studies from Alice Deal Middle School in Washington. By now, he had become used to Washington's ambience. During this period he had established his newspaper business by distributing 'Washington Post' and other papers and magazines. As far as his studies were concerned he was an average student.

In June, 1943 the 13 year old Warren along with two friends, ran away from his home in Fredericksburg, Virginia and reached a place called Hershey in Pennsylvania. There they wanted to work as Caddy's in the golf course. They spent the night in a hotel in Hershey. Next day some policemen made enquiries from them and after being satisfied by their replies, left. After this, the boys also decided to return home.

His father, therefore, placed a conditional challenge before him – either get better marks or shut down the newspaper business.

Warren loved making money, so he concentrated not only on his studies over the next several months and improved his performance; he also expanded his newspaper business. He started delivering 5 newspapers and magazines. Any customer who did not want the 'Washington Post', he would offer 'Times Harold' to them. By 1945, he was earning 175 dollars a month. This amount was equivalent to many grown-ups monthly salary.

In the same year when he went to Omaha during summer with his family, merely at the age of 14 he decided to buy 40 acres of farmland in Nebraska. From the newspaper business earnings he bought the land for 1200 dollars and rented it out to a farmer. It was beginning of the career of the world's most successful investor.

Warren Edward Buffett was born on 30th August, 1930 in Omaha. From his father's side, his ancestors were Huguenots from France, who had moved to America in 1600. For the next 250 years they did farming in Huntington in Long Island. One of them Sidney Homan Buffett decided to move to the west to start a new life. This was in the year 1867, when the civil war had ended and America was expanding towards the West. Sydney reached the main town Omaha. He saw wooden houses by the side of Missouri river and flat land beyond. He started working as a stage coach driver and later opened S.H. Buffett grocery store.

Only three months earlier the country's east and west regions had been connected by train. There was two way movement of people between the east and west parts of the country. In 1970, people had started arriving and settling in Omaha. Houses with steel structures were also being built and even an Opera House had been built. Consequently, Omaha town was growing and so was the business of S.H. Buffett grocery store. The store was supplying provisions of all kinds from flour to salt in hotels, restaurants and homes.

In the year 1900, the population of Omaha had grown to 1,40,000. Sydney Buffett expanded his store. He also got married; he had two sons, who started helping him in his business. In 1915, one of his sons Ernest opened another store named 'Buffett and Sons' in the newly developing western part of the town. The affluent people of Omaha were developing this part of the town.

Ernest got married and had a son, who was named Howard. It was expected that after Howard grew up, he will manage the family business, but he had no interest in business. He did not want to manage the grocery store. As a student at Nebraska University in Lincoln his inclination for journalism was growing and he became the editor of 'Daily Nebraska.' There he met a simple girl named Leila Stahl, whose father was publisher for a weekly paper in the suburbs of Nebraska. The 16 year old Leila had completed her high school and was looking for a job in a newspaper, so that she could meet her college expenses. She had gained good experience in journalism. When she was in 5th class, she had started helping her father in his weekly paper's work. She herself would compose the matter and even operate the linotype machine. She could conduct interviews and even write the articles nicely. Every Thursday she would operate the printing machine and print the paper.

Howard employed her and also fell in love with her. They got married on 26th December, 1925. By then Howard had completed his college studies. Even though he had wanted to work as a journalist, but when a friend of his father proposed him a job in an insurance company, he accepted it. After this job, Howard got a job in Union Street Bank, where he was assigned the responsibility for selling shares.

In 1928 Leila gave birth to a daughter, who was named Doris. Two years later on 30th August, 1930 Warren was born. That day it rained and the rain cooled the 89 degrees Fahrenheit heat.

Within a year, two weeks before Warren's first birthday the bank where his father used to work closed down. In 1924, when recession set in, countless American companies became bankrupt. Consequently, Howard Buffett also lost his job and exhausted all his savings.

Howard was a determined, hard working person who was dedicated towards his goal. He started a new business with a colleague. He started trading in investment securities, Municipal Corporation and public utilities stock and bonds. He earned commission on their sales. The commission was not much and it was uncertain. Howard and his colleague were also inexperienced in the securities trading. Moreover, when the population of Nebraska was finding it difficult to meet two ends, they could not think of investing. The poor farmers were constrained to eat in charitable messes.

Leila was fulfilling her responsibilities as a housewife with due care, keeping in mind his husband's limited income. Several times she would feed her husband and children and go to bed without eating. However, gradually their financial condition started improving. When Warren was three years old his younger sister Roberta was born. When Warren was six years old his father bought a large mansion on 53rd street in North Omaha and the entire family moved there.

Bottle Caps and Golf Balls

When Warren started going to school, his parents realised that he was born with a fascination for numbers and capabilities to earn money. At the age of five, he set up a kiosk in front of his house and started selling Chicklet bubble gum to the passersby. At the age of six when he went for holidays with his family by a lake side in Iowa, he found out that he could buy a pack of six cokes for a quarter. He sold a single bottle of coke at a time for a nickel to the visiting tourists, thus he earned a profit of 5 cents after selling six bottles of coke. After he returned to Omaha, during his summer holidays, he started earning money by buying soft drinks from his grandfather's store and selling them in the neighbourhood.

When Warren was nine years old, his mother saw that he was collecting bottle caps from a vending machine located in a gas agency near his friend Bob Russell's house. He and Bob counted the brand-wise soft drinks bottle caps to know which soft drink brand was selling the most. At the same time, they started collecting the usable golf balls from Omaha Country Club. They would sell such balls. Warren's mother saw different brand golf ball stored in separate baskets, in his bedroom. Each basket was labelled with the brand name of the golf ball and its price. Warren starting selling the golf balls through his friends and started earning commission on it.

When he was not busy on the golf course he would go to the Ak-Sar-Ben racetrack. He would collect any useful thing he found thrown near the betting window and the grand stand. He would earn some profit from such collection also.

As a child Warren's favourite game was to study the symbols of corporate stocks and bonds. These symbols were marked on the ticker tape, which his father used to bring home from his brokerage office. Warren had memorized hundreds of symbols. Warren would also study in-depth the stock and bond certificates available in large numbers in his father's office. Warren was a welcome visitor in the office of a neighbourhood brokerage firm 'Harris Upham', because he would note down the current stock prices on their blackboard accurately.

Thereafter he started making chart of the movement of different share prices at his home only. When he was 11 years old, he decided to buy 3 shares of, 'Cites Service

Preferred', at 38 dollars per share, in his and his sister Doris's name. The share quickly dropped to 27 dollars a share and then gradually rose to 40 dollars a share. Warren immediately sold the shares. After deducting the commission on the trade his father gave him, he earned his first profit of 5 dollars in the share market. He sold the shares at a small profit but regretted his decision when the share rose to 200 dollars. He learnt his lesson of patience in investing.

Warren and his friend Bob Russell would spend hours playing mental games. For instance, they would keep record of how many times some words appeared in a newspaper. They would learn details about different towns, thereafter Bob would name the town and Warren would immediately tell the total population of the town and so on. Bob would ask him questions on the history of baseball and Warren would start narrating the players betting averages and other team details. On Sundays in the Church, his mother would watch him preparing the age records of the people who had written the prayers.

Warren would enjoy spending time in Bob's house. Whereas Warren's house was located in a quite locality, Bob's house was located in a crowded locality. There was constant traffic jams in that area. Once Warren said to Mrs. Russell, "This area is so much crowded, it is a matter of shame that you are not making any money here in spite of so much traffic of people".

Warren and Bob started learning mathematical formulas. Pretty soon they developed a mathematical technique, which could help in betting on the race course. After testing their technique at the Ak-Sar-Ben racetrack, they were convinced that they could make money at the betting window. For the next race they brought out a hand written horseracing tip sheet called, 'Stable Boy Selection'. While they were selling the tip sheet, they were told by the Officers that a license was required for selling it. But as they were under age, they could not get the license. So they had to stop it.

In Washington D.C.

In 1942, there was a major turn in Warren's life. On 7th December, 1941, the Japanese bombed Pearl Harbour, which sucked America into World War II. The Democratic President Franklin Delano Roosevelt was so popular that in 1940, he was elected President for the third time in a row. The Republican's of Omaha were on the lookout of a candidate who could defeat the Democratic candidate for the Representative election. They selected Omaha's businessman Howard Buffett, who was well-known for being critical of Roosevelt's current policies.

Many persons including his father wanted that Howard should win the Representative elections. Howard won the election. Twelve year old Warren had to pack his bags and baggage, bid his friends goodbye with whom he had spent joyous days. He had to move to Washington D.C. with his family. Washington D.C. being the capital city had become overcrowded on account of the war. So the Warren family had to rent a house in the suburbs in Fredericksburg, Virginia.

Now his father, with whom Warren had a closer attachment as compared to his mother, was staying in a hotel room in Washington D.C. He would visit his family only at the weekends. Warren was desperately missing Omaha and he expressed his inner turmoil in a letter, which he wrote to his grandfather Ernest. His grandfather wrote back that he could stay with him and his Aunt Alice in Omaha, till he completed his 8th class studies. Warren's parents agreed to send him to Omaha.

Warren returned to Omaha and was pleased to meet his friends. During the next four months, while studying to complete his 8th class, he would roam around the western areas of Omaha on a motorbike. After returning from school and on holidays his grandfather would ask him to work in his store 'Buffett and Sons.' He soon learnt to successfully manage the business. He would arrange the stock on the shelves, clean the fruit and vegetable baskets and even pick up the heavy items. He did not very much like these types of jobs and could not tolerate the smell of the groceries. Yet he liked arranging the stock on racks placed against the wall and handing over the items asked by the customers. He learnt a basic lesson that for a business to be successful, one must always remain busy. He had observed that all the workers in the store were constantly busy day or night.

On his way to school, frequently Warren would have lunch at his father's business partner Carl Falk's house. There one day he told Mrs. Falk that he wanted to become a millionaire before he turned 30 years old.

Mrs. Falk asked him, "Warren why do you want to earn so much money?"

The 13 years old guest Warren answered, "It is not as if I only want to earn money, I enjoy earning money and its growth pleases me."

□

5

From Golf Course to Graduate School

In September 1943, after bidding goodbye to his dear grandfather and Aunt Alice, Warren returned to Washington. There he joined Alice Dale Junior High School for his 9th class studies. His parents had moved to a house on 49th Street in Washington. The house was located in the north-west district of the city, next to Massachusetts Avenue.

Warren, who was always eager to earn money, started distributing the 'Washington Post', newspaper door-to-door. He used to get up early and complete the distribution of the newspaper before it was time to go to school. Yet he was not at all happy to stay in Washington. He was younger than his classmates. While studying in Omaha, he had moved one class higher. He had very few friends in Washington. His school principal had warned his mother about his shabby dressing habits and asked her that she should send him to school properly dressed. By June Warren had turned to be a young man who could defy conventional set up and rules.

This was the time when Warren had run away to Hershey along with his two friends. He was sure that they will get caddy's job in the golf course there. However, after they were questioned by the policeman the next morning, Warren decided to return home. When he returned home his father clearly told him, 'Either secure good marks or stop selling the newspaper.' This had the desired effect on Warren who did not want to stop the newspaper business.

By winter, his teachers also felt that Warren was concentrating on his studies and there was improvement in the marks secured by him. On the other hand, the circulation Manager of 'Washington Post', had also tied up with the fourteen year old Warren to sell more copies of the newspaper. By now Warren was selling approximately 500 copies in five localities. He had to put in a lot of effort to distribute the newspaper in apartment blocks. He would take the lift up to the 4th floor in an 8 floor building, leave half of the newspapers there, take the balance newspapers up to the 8th floor and deliver the newspaper to each apartment using the staircase.

'Times Harold', newspaper was a competitor of 'Washington Post.' Warren took up the distribution of this newspaper also. When a customer discontinued 'Washington Post' then Warren would persuade him to subscribe to 'Harold Times.' In addition he was supplying magazines also. By the summer of 1944, he was earning approximately 175 dollars a month through the newspaper and magazine business.

In November 1944, Warren's father was elected to the House of Representatives for the second time. At that time Warren was studying for his 10th class in Washington's Woodrow Wilson High School. He was making new friends and was playing golf for his school team. He and his friends would collect the thrown golf balls. They would clean and sell them. One friend of Warren, Donald Denali used to play the piano. He also enjoyed playing number game like Warren. They would play the number games for hours, without using any paper or pencil. They would question each other and solve them orally, even the two digit multiplications.

Pin Ball Machines and Tennis Shoes

Donald had expertise in repairing broken machines. In the spring of 1946, while studying for his senior grade, Donald bought an old pin ball machine for 25 dollars. He repaired it and made it operational. Warren and Donald operated it repeatedly but it broke down every time. However, Donald was able to repair it every time. When Warren saw that Donald was able to repair the machine every time with ease, he suggested that they hire it out to the barbers shop in the neighbourhood.

The barber agreed to keep the machine in the shop provided it earned him a decent income. On the first day there was an earning of 14 dollars. Within a month Warren and Donald hired out seven machines in such shops and started earning 50 dollars a week. They named their company, 'Wilson Coin Operated Machine Company.' They had named their company prompted by the name of their school. Warren had bought the used machines between 25 to 75 dollars. On the other hand, Donald would service the complaints. He would reach the shop on his motorbike. They would introduce themselves as employees of a large business corporation.

Several years later Warren had told that, "The owners of the barber shops would demand for new machines and we would assure them that we shall inform the higher officials about it. We would pretend that we were salaried employees and our job was to provide the machines and manage the cash".

Many years later Warren's high school classmates still remembered a particular thing about him, "We often joked that Warren would only wear tennis shoes, howsoever, cold it might be."

Another friend said, "We would frequently make fun of him about it. He would wear the same shoes round the year. Even when there was knee deep snow he would not feel any difficulty in moving around wearing his tennis shoes."

At home, 16 year old Warren was fond of his father, who in November 1946 successively for the third time won the Representative election from Nebraska. Warren was aware that his father had a conservative attitude. When he was appointed for the first time as Representative, then the Representative's had decided to enhance their salary from 10,000 dollars to 12,500 dollars. His father had protested against the enhancement stating that the people had appointed him as their Representative on a salary of 10,000 dollars, so he will not accept the higher pay.

It was almost time for Warren to enter college. His father suggested that he should seek admission in Pennsylvania University's Horton School of Finance and Commerce. Warren said, "There was no need for him to study any further. He had already earned more than 5,000 dollars by selling 600,000 copies of newspapers. He was earning a regular income from the pin ball machines and the 40 acres land purchased in Nebraska. He had already read more than 100 books on business topics. What new things could any school teach him about business?"

His father reminded him that he was not even 17 years old. Warren hesitantly agreed to seek admission in Horton School.

In the June of 1947 Warren completed his high schooling from Woodrow Wilson High School and secured 16th position out of 347 students. In the Wilson year book, below his photograph was the caption– 'Likes mathematics, a future stock broker.'

When his friend Donald Denali's girl friend asked him if he was going to settle in Washington, then Warren replied, "No, I will settle in Omaha."

Rolls Royce Ride

After taking admission in Horton, Warren soon

realised that what he had thought was right and told his father so. No Professor knew more than what he had already learned. During holidays when he returned to Omaha, his father's business partner's wife Mary Falk asked him whether he was concentrating on his studies or not?

He replied, "All I have to do is to open my books and empty a large bottle of coke on the eve of the examination. I shall secure 100 per cent marks."

After spending a year in Horton, when he returned to Washington during summer holidays, he had already made up his mind to discontinue his studies. His father, however, convinced him to continue with his studies for the second year also. During this period he would ride in his friend Donald's Roll Royce car all through Washington. Donald had purchased this 1928 model car from a scrap dealer. He had repaired the car and painted it deep blue colour. Just for fun sake, Donald would don a chauffer's uniform, whereas Warren and Donald's girl friend would dress as a rich couple and occupy the back seat. They would then drive through Washington's affluent areas. Donald would stop the car anywhere in-between, open the hood of the car and pretend to examine it. After some time when a crowd of curious onlookers gathered, Warren would get down from the car and point his cane towards any part of the engine. Donald would then pretend to repair that part, after which all of them would carry on with their drive.

In Horton, Warren used to stay at a friend's house, where he would be engrossed in very challenging games of bridge. He would freely chat with his friends. One of his friend told, "He was a very funny boy. He was very clever. Whenever he was with us, he would make us laugh."

Weekend beer parties were held at his friend's place. Many of Warren's classmates had become his pals just to drink free beer. Warren himself used to drink only Pepsi-cola. In the party, Warren's ideas on politics and economics used to impress everyone. They had realised that Warren's knowledge was much more extensive than their own knowledge. Compared to his Professors dull lectures, Warren could talk in a more interesting way. One of his classmates told, "Warren had realised that there was nothing new which he could learn at Horton. I think, he was right."

In November 1948, Howard Buffett lost the Representative election and returned to Omaha with his wife and daughters. In June 1949, Warren completed his second year term at Horton and took admission in Nebraska University in Lincoln for his further studies. He never looked back but later he told, "I always had the feeling that I was not learning much."

50 Hawkers and 2,640 Golf Balls

After studying for 2 years at Horton, Warren decided to complete his Bachelor's degree in 3 years instead of 4 years. In the winter of 1949, Warren started studying five syllabuses of economics and business, whereas the scheduled starting time was 1950. During this time he also took up a job in the newspaper, 'Lincoln Journal.' He became the supervisor of 50 hawkers in the 6 rural districts of Nebraska. He used to get 75 cents per hour. In the afternoons, he would tour his area in a car and reappoint new hawkers.

In the winter of 1950, Warren decided to restart his golf balls business. He appointed Jerry, a classmate from Horton as his sales agent in Philadelphia and started supplying him used golf balls. By July, he sold 2640 balls and earned 1,200 dollars. After the summer holidays he returned home and started studying three syllabuses in the Omaha precinct of Nebraska University for his degree. By then he had earned 9,800 dollars from the newspaper job and sale of golf balls.

Thereafter Warren applied for admission in Harvard Business School. Nineteen year old Warren was called to Chicago for the interview. The interview lasted for 10 minutes only. Later Warren told, "The snoot nosed interviewers at Harvard thought that I was under aged and so they asked me to wait for one or two years."

But Warren could not wait. He applied for admission in New York's Columbia University Graduate School of Business. One of the Professor of Columbia University, Professor Benjamin Graham had written the book 'Intelligent Investor', which Warren had read and liked it very much. Professor Benjamin could never have known that very soon he would become lifelong guide of a 19 year old inquisitive youth.

□

6
Intelligent Investor

The title of Benjamin Graham's book, 'Intelligent Investor', aptly describes as to what Warren had wanted to become in life. Warren used to constantly ponder about Investors. People used to buy shares of proprietary companies and hoped that they would make some profit. Warren liked Graham's fundamental advice that an intelligent investor should not blindly follow the other Wall Street investors. Instead Graham had advised in his book that the investor should invest in companies which were trading below their intrinsic value.

According to Graham, it was not easy to identify such companies. It required a lot of patience. It was necessary to study every aspect of the working of the company- its assets, its earnings and its future plans. After conducting such an analysis the investor could determine the true price of the share of the company, in other words the price, which had no relation to the price being quoted in the share market.

Graham believed the prices in the market were like a popularity contest. The prices reflected the sentiments of the investors towards that company. The movement of share prices in the share market was often based on rumours and false propaganda and they may have no relationship with the facts. One could not decide the correct price of the share of any company on the basis of prices quoted in the market.

Graham had concluded that the intelligent investor should buy the shares of any company when they are trading below their intrinsic value. Thereafter, the investor should patiently wait for the share price to rise. It is definite that the share price would rise sooner or later.

After reading the book Warren discovered the mantra of investing. He was impressed by the basic rules described by Graham. While buying shares from his father's brokerage or while studying in Horton from a brokerage in Philadelphia, Warren followed these basic rules. He saw that the people who bought shares on rumours or on guess work had to face the uncertainties of the share market. He firmly believed that by buying share on guess work could never earn any profit for the investor. He believed that this practice was totally wrong.

In September, 1950 Warren was one of twenty students who were studying in Graham's class. He was quite impressed by Graham's style of teaching. Graham never used to accept or reject instantly the reply of any student, to the queried question. Instead he would ask, "On what basis have you arrived at this conclusion?"

Graham would teach his students how to study and analyse the annual report of a company; how to determine the true value of its share based on its financial statement. He would present two balance sheets of two purportedly different companies to the students for comparison. Later, he would dramatically disclose that the balance sheets were of the same airplanes manufacturing company-Boeing; but of different periods. He was in fact training the students of the manner in which the companies preferred to disclose their information for record. The students can determine the true value of its shares based on the information provided on record only.

Warren was imbibing the knowledge into his blood streams. He had answer to all the questions. Later, one of his classmates told, "He would frequently raise his hand to reply and he would participate in the discussions enthusiastically. He possessed amazing zeal. As compared to others, he would always speak without any hesitation."

He was greatly impressed by his Professor's intelligence and friendly nature; so he wanted to compile all the available information on him. During his second semester at Columbia, he came to know that Graham was the Head of the Government Employees Insurance Company G.E.I.C.O. Its headquarter was in Washington D.C.

In November 1950, his father Howard Buffett again won the Representative election, after remaining out of the House of Representatives for two years. In 1951, Warren joined his family in Washington for a week's holiday. He arrived at Washington railway station on a Saturday morning and the same day he went to the headquarter of G.E.I.C.O. located on K Street. There he met a guard and told him that he wanted to meet an Officer of the Company. He was introduced to the Deputy Finance Officer Lorimer A. Davidson. An unknown young man posed numerous questions to Davidson.

Later Davidson told, "After talking to him for 15 minutes, I realised that the stranger was not an ordinary person. He was asking intelligent questions based on the facts. What is G.E.I.C.O.? How did it conduct his business, what are its objectives, what are its growth prospects? He was asking questions which could have only been raised by an experienced investor. He wanted to gain all the information which I had."

Both talked for about 4 hours. Warren came to know that two persons from Texas, Leo Goodwin, Sr. and Lillian Goodwin had founded G.E.I.C.O., who planned to sell insurance policies directly to Government Employees. Government Employees claims were much less than any other group of persons. Direct sales also meant that there was no need to pay any commission to agents.

□

7

Life Partner

The young Warren used to stay away from girls. Even though he desired that he had a girl friend, but his attitude would become a hindrance. Later he said, "In the presence of girls, no one was as shy as I was. Maybe I was hesitant in continuing a conversation." Except for talking about shares and politics, he had little else to talk about. He felt nervous in asking a girl out for a date. In school or college, he could not mix freely with girls. His limited interactions with girls were not very pleasant.

While going out to witness a baseball game with a girl named Jackie Gideon, his car crashed against a cow. While he had gone out with another girl, he got hit by a golf ball. While he had gone out with a girl named Ann Beck, he kept sitting in front of her but could not utter a single word, as if he was a mute. He could not decide if she would like to hear him speak about Ben Graham. A girl named Bunny Merlin tried to befriend Warren for many days but nothing came out of it.

Finally in the summer of 1950 before he left for California his sister Berty introduced him to her roommate Susan Thompson. She came from the North-Western part of the country and was a cute girl with a round chin. She had impressed Berty at once, who was one and half years younger than her. Berty was an expert in understanding people. When Warren met Susan, he was enamoured by her; but somehow he doubted her appearance.

"I can most certainly say that in the beginning she was acting. I was impressed by her and was trying to attract her; but I also wanted to know her real self. I could not believe that there could be any girl like that in reality."

In fact Susan was not attracted towards Warren, as she was in love with someone else.

After leaving Columbia Warren read in the Earl Wilson's gossip column in, 'New York Post', that the year 1949 'Miss Nebraska' Vanita Brown was staying in Webster Women's Residence. She was participating in a T.V. show with singer and idol of the youngsters Eddy Fisher.

Vanita was studying in Nebraska University, when Warren was also studying there. Even though, till now he had not specifically noticed her and since the glamorous Miss Nebraska was staying in New York, he called her at the Webster residence. Gradually Warren had been overcoming his shyness.

Vanita decided to meet him and try her luck. They had met once in the past. Warren knew that she had been brought up in totally different circumstances. She had grown up in the neighbourhood of the southern Omaha's storages, where after returning from school she used to skin chickens in Omaha Cold Storage. Her shapely body and intoxicating face attracted lots of people. She got her first job in Paramount Theatre. Then she participated in the local beauty contests.

"I think her real talent lied in charming the judges." Warren said.

After winning the 'Miss Nebraska' title, Vanita participated in the beauty contest in Washington D.C. Thereafter she came to New York and tried to establish herself in the show business there.

Even though she knew that Warren was not a boy who would take a girl to a stark club or to cope cabana for a show; yet she welcomed the boy from her home town warmly. Pretty soon they were seen roaming about on the streets of New York. Both of them started visiting the Marble Collegiate Church to listen to the lectures of Norman Vincent Peel on personality development. Peel had written several books on personality development and was a powerful orator.

Warren used to take Vanita by the side of Hudson River for cheese sandwiches. Even though Vanita did not like cheese sandwiches but she wanted to retain her relationship with Warren. Warren found her entertaining and witty. While talking to Vanita he felt the same pleasure as if he was playing oral ping-pong. Vanita's beauty had its own charm. In spite of Vanita's company Warren could not fully develop the art of mixing freely in society. As time passed, he became increasingly concerned about this shortcoming in his personality. He saw an advertisement offering a course on the Dale Carnegie style of speaking. Warren had lot of faith in Dale Carnegie who had mastered the techniques of 'How to win friends and influence people.' He reached the institute in New York to join the course with a 100 dollar cheque in his pocket.

"I went to join the Dale Carnegie public speaking course because I was facing difficulty in mixing socially. I gave the cheque, but then I stopped its payment because I changed my mind."

During winter, Warren kept on writing letters to Susan Thompson. But there was no improvement in their relationship. She neither prompted him to write nor told him to stop writing. Warren thought that if he met Susan's parents it might help him to get closer to her. Warren went with Susan's parents to see a football match in West Side and then went out for dinner with them. But during dinner Susan left them to meet a friend.

After spending his holidays, Warren returned to New York. He felt a little handicapped there, but did not give up hope. In the meanwhile he kept meeting Vanita.

Later Warren said, "Of all the people I met, Vanita was the most imaginative girl."

In fact becoming intimate with Vanita was like giving invitation to uncertainty and insecurity. She had threatened Warren several times that she will go to Washington and when Howard Buffett was addressing the House of Representatives; she will kneel down on her knees in front of him and scream, 'Warren is the father of the child in my womb.' Warren was apprehensive of her carrying out the threat. Once she created such an ugly scene in the cinema hall that Warren had to drag her out of the cinema hall and left without her.

Vanita was beautiful and bewitching. But she was hot-headed and dangerous. Warren had realised that getting closer to her could be perilous. But Warren felt an exhilarating pleasure in retaining her friendship. It was like taming a tigress.

"Vanita could take care of herself. She could do so quite easily. The question was whether she wanted to do it or not? She was not a nuisance for others unless she so desired."

Once Warren arranged a dinner party in New York Athletic Club, in the honour of a distinguished Lawyer and Navy's Secretary Frank Mathews and also invited Vanita. He thought that the presence of the beautiful Miss Nebraska will add glamour to the party. Mathew himself was a resident of Nebraska. The other invitees were also well-known personalities of the society. Warren wanted to impress the guests. However, while cocktails were being served Vanita embarrassed Warren. When Warren introduced her as a friend, she contradicted him and said that she was his wife. She said, "I don't know why he is feeling embarrassed in telling the truth? Whenever he takes me out he says that I am his friend; whereas the fact is that we are married."

Eventually Warren understood that Vanita could take care of herself, but, "In reality she could always create difficulties for me and she always enjoyed acting in a whimsical manner," Warren told later. She would often behave whimsically. She had a superiority complex and had no inkling as how she would behave at any particular moment.

Whenever Warren visited his home in Nebraska, he would meet Susan Thompson. Even these meetings were brief. He thought that she was cultured, imposing and compassionate. Warren later told, "As compared to me, she was much more mature."

His attraction for Susan was getting stronger, so he started looking for ways to distance himself from Vanita. Warren later told, "Even though I knew that I was not her first love, but I was convinced that it was not going to affect our relations."

Susan's family and Buffett family knew each other quite well. In fact it was Susan's father, William Thompson who had managed Howard Buffett's election campaign for the fourth term, which Howard lost. In spite of the acquaintance, there were a lot of dissimilarities between the two families. Susan's mother Dorothy Thompson was a sweet natured, courteous, generous and erudite woman, who always fulfilled her obligations towards her family consciously. She would ensure that dinner was served on the dinning table exactly at 6 O'clock in the evening. She fully assisted her husband Dr. William Thompson, so that he could manage his busy schedule smoothly. William Thompson always formally dressed in a suit and would move around as if everyone was praising him.

He was the Dean of the Arts and Science College of Omaha University. He also taught psychology and as the Assistant Athletic Director was responsible for the athletic activities of the University also. As a former football player and sports lover he used to be involved in all the activities enthusiastically. Warren told later, "His role made him so famous in the town that all the policemen recognized him, which was a boon for him as he was a rather careless driver." He had also designed IQ and psychology tests for the students. He was especially interested in conducting examinations for the town's school children. He did not like spending even a single holiday at home, away from his hectic schedule. On Sundays, he would give sermons in the Church, in an earnest but soft voice. His two daughters gave him company by singing hymns. In the remaining time he would discuss his political beliefs in different groups of people. His political beliefs were more or less similar to the political beliefs of Howard Buffett.

Whenever William Thompson would ask for anything, it was meant to be taken as an order. He used to talk about the pride of women, but he himself disregarded it. He used to study in-depth the psychology of mankind, but he was unable to properly understand their sentiments. He wanted to see the people whom he liked, to remain close to him. He used to be disturbed if he did not see them around. He felt that his dear ones might get into unexpected troubles. He used to adore people who followed his advice as directed.

Thompson's elder daughter, Dotty was temperamentally averse to following his orders. According to the family members, in Dotty's initial years when her father had become extremely annoyed with her, he used to lock her in the cupboard.

His second daughter Susan was born seven years after Dotty's birth. Mother Dorothy was shaken by the father's behaviour towards her elder daughter Dotty, so she told her husband, "The elder daughter is yours, I will bring up the younger daughter as I choose.

Susie was a sickly child from birth. She was troubled by her allergy and ear infection. In the first eighteen months her ear had to be cleaned a dozen times. She was fever prone. In the second grade of kindergarten, she was confined to her home for four to five months due to her sickness. Later, she told that she used to watch her friends playing from the window and feel annoyed with herself.

Her parents used to pay special attention towards her on account of her sickness. Warren had said "Susie could do no wrong, whereas faults were found in everything Dotty did. Nobody treated her properly."

Even after Susie recovered and there was no need for her to be confined, she showed no interest in going out to play. Instead she took special interest in making new friends because she was completely isolated from everyone, on account of her sickness.

Later Susie reminisced, "After you suffer pain, relief from it provides an amazing feeling of freedom. The feeling is just fantastic. Relief from pain heals your heart. I understood this at my tender age itself. This realization changes your outlook towards life and it becomes simplistic. Then while developing new acquaintances all that comes to your mind is how good the people are."

Susie was growing up. Her round chin was very attractive. Her babyish voice used to impulsively draw attention towards her. In her teens, she took admission in Omaha's Central High School. Students from different sections of the society used to study together in this school, which was a very unusual thing for the forties. Even though she used to mix with the elite group, yet all her classmates remembered her as popular and simple student. The kind of intensity she used to display and used to open her heart innocently easily impressed people. She was more interested in oration and performing arts instead of being immersed in studies. In debating competitions, she would present her views confidently and sincerely. People noticed that her ideology was mostly opposite to her father's ideology. In the school plays, she used to act forcefully and in musical shows she would sing melodiously. Many of her musical shows became memorable events for the audience. The magnetism of her personality had impressed everyone in the school and her classmates elected her, 'Senior Class President.'

Susie's first boyfriend was a pleasant boy named John Gilmore whom she liked very much. While studying at Central High School even though John was one feet taller than Susie, she used to dominate her.

During that period she made a new friend, an intelligent boy whom she had met in a debating competition. Milton Brown was a student of Thomas Jefferson High School in Council Slough, Iowa. He had an enticing smile. He was a tall, dark haired pleasant boy. They would meet frequently. Susie's close friends were aware of her friendship with Milton. Her friendship with Gilmore was also intact and she would attend parties and school functions with him.

Susie's father did not like Milton Brown, who was the son of an illiterate Russian-Jew immigrant labourer and used to work on the Labour Union Pacific Railway Track. Susie took him to her home three or four times. Her father was rude to Brown and used to lecture him on FDR and Truman. Her father was against her daughter's friendship with a Jew boy and never bothered to hide his negative feelings towards him. Susie's father also used to believe in Omaha's conventional family traditions like the Buffett family. He was not prepared to deviate from this traditional thinking. But Susie was trying to cross over the traditional social boundaries. Yet in high school, she was popular for following traditions.

Facing such dilemmas, for her college studies Susie took admission in North Western University in Winston, Illinois. Milton was also studying there. There they both felt the sense of having freedom. Susie shared her room with Berty Buffett. While studying for Journalism, Susie planned her schedule so that she had time to meet Milton every day.

Milton was doing odd jobs to fund his studies. Susie and Milton would meet in the library. Students of her community were not happy to see her getting close to a Jew boy. They were particularly annoyed when she took him along for a dance performance. Even though she was hurt by this treatment, she did not stop seeing Milton. They both started learning 'Baudh Dharma', to attain mental peace.

During this time unaware of all these happenings, Warren went to Winston to see a football match and in the winter holidays went to Omaha to meet Susie. By then he had made up his mind to express his affection to her. She had all the qualities which Warren wanted to see in a woman. But it was Milton Brown on whom she wanted to shower her affection.

In 1951, Milton was elected 'Class President' and Berty Buffett elected 'Vice-President'. Susie would weep while reading letters from home which directed her to terminate her relationship with Milton. Berty could only watch her shedding tears emotionally as Susie never shared her feelings with her. It seemed as if she wanted to keep others out of the emotional trauma which she was undergoing. Just before the session ended, Susie's father directed her over phone to return home. When she reached Omaha her father told her that she could not see Milton under any circumstances and she could also not go back to North Western University. Susie's world came crashing down and she started weeping bitterly. But her father did not relent.

At that time, Warren had also returned to Omaha after completing his graduation from Columbia. Warren's parents were living in Washington at that time and Warren was to stay in his parental home. He also had to serve time with the National Guards for some time during the summer holidays. Even though he was not fully fit to join the National Guards but it was a better option than fighting war in Korea. Every year he had also to attend the training camp in La Crosse Wisconsin for a few weeks. Even after attending such training camps he had not matured.

"In the National Guards the other boys would eye me suspiciously because my Dad was a Congressman. They thought that I was a strange animal. But this belief was short-lived. The organization was established on core democratic values. What I mean is that it does not matter what you are outside. Here to develop team spirit you must even be prepared for reading comics. I was reading comics within the hour of reaching there. When the others were doing the same, how could I be different? Four words were added to my vocabulary, which I am sure you can easily guess."

"I learnt that when you are in the company of people who are better than you then you also develop. Whereas when you are in the company of people who are inferior to you then it quickly leads to your downfall."

After returning from the training camp, based on his experience Warren said, "I use to hesitate while speaking to a group. You will not believe the state of my mind I used to be when it was my turn to address the group. I was so scared that I could not even utter a single word. I wished that I should somehow disappear. In fact, I had designed my life-style so that I need not speak in front of others. When I returned to Omaha after completing my graduation, I saw an advertisement. I knew that at some point of time, I will have to speak in front of others. I was terribly scared of this thought, so to overcome this fright, I enrolled for the art of speaking course.

This however, was not the single objective which he had in mind. He understood that to win over Susan Thompson's affection, it was necessary for him to be able to talk to her freely and leave a lasting impression. Earlier on several occasions, he had stammered while talking to her.

He was prepared to do anything to improve his shortcoming and also knew that this year's summer holidays were his last chance to do so.

Dale Carnegie's public speaking classes were held in Hotel Rome, which was the favourite spot of the shepherds.

"I took the fees for the course with me, which I paid to the Instructor were Poly Kennan and told him to keep it before I changed my mind. There twenty-five to thirty students. We were all perturbed. We could not even pronounce our names. We all stood there but were unable to talk to each other. I was, however, impressed by Poly Kennan's ability to remember names of all the students and the ease with which he called our names. He was a good teacher and he used to teach us the tricks to sharpen our memory; but I was unable to learn them. We were given copies of keynote speeches, election speeches, Lt. Governor's speech etc. to memorise and it was expected that we will be able to narrate the speeches. This would motivate us to overcome our hesitation. Why is it that you do not hesitate to talk freely to a single person, but are unable to utter even a single in front of a group? He used to teach us psychological tricks to overcome our fear. We had to practice some of these tricks. We were helping each other to overcome our hesitation. It had helped me quite a bit by the time I completed the course."

However, Warren did not use this ability on Susie. He understood that Susie was influenced by her father, so he was thinking of ways to impress him, when he was alone. William Thompson liked to play the mandolin in his garden during summer. Warren would sing sitting in front of him. Susie would then quietly leave to meet Milton.

Warren liked to spend time with William Thompson. In his company, he was reminded of his father, who blamed the Democrats for all the wrongs. Like Warren's father, William was also interested in discussing sporting activities, in addition to politics. He had no son and he considered Warren to be the perfect future son-in-law. Warren was hot-blooded, was a Protestant, was a Republican and most importantly Warren was not Milton Brown.

But William's acceptance was not enough to bring him closer to Susie. In spite of lot of efforts, Warren could not win over Susie's affection. She might have overlooked his loose socks and cheap dress, but his other qualities did not impress her as well. He was a Congressman's son, who had a special status in the society. He was a graduate with handsome savings and was progressing rapidly. He would always talk about shares. It was a topic in which Susie had no interest. During his outings with Susan, he would narrate memorized jokes, quiz riddles and ask her questions to test mental ability. Since William liked Warren, she saw her father's personality's reflection in him. William had almost forced Susie to be with Warren. Warren later told, "It was one against two."

Milton liked Susie and he needed him also but since he was a Jew, he had to face injustice. He was a handsome youth, but Susie's father disliked him.

That year during summer, Milton Brown was working for Council Sloughs. He received information from North Western University regarding hike of fees; he realized that he will not go to Evanston for further studies. So he handed over a letter to Berty Buffett, in which he had written that he was going to take admission in Iowa University. That year Susie was taking admission in Omaha University. By then both of them realized that their paths were separated on account of Susie's father's interference. Susie spent the summer holidays weeping.

On the other hand, in spite of her initial dislike for Warren, Susie could not spend time with him without knowing everything about him. She soon realized that her initial impression about Warren was not right. Warren was not what she had thought– Warren was not a pampered young man, full of self-confidence.

"I was confused." Warren told later. He needed support. "I could not understand my state of mind. I was not able to mix socially. In addition till now I had not experienced a fast paced life." Susie's friends were also feeling that the overtly confident Warren was inertly restlessness. Gradually, Susie also started understanding that he was lonely. Even though he would talk fascinating things about shares, but in fact he was in search of love, as he was lonely. He was like a child in search of a safe place. Later Warren said, "I was confused. The wonderful thing was that Susie had perceived the state of my mind."

Warren was not bothered how others dressed. He was not even attracted by the attire of women. But now since he was deeply in love with Susie, he particularly started noticing her dresses. He remembered going out with Susie in a blue dress. Also when she was dressed in a black and white dress, he had called it a 'newspaper dress'. They were dancing on the dance floor of Peony Park Pavilion. Warren had not learnt dancing, so he was somehow trying to match the steps. He was blushing like a child on the dance floor. Later he said, "I was ready to do whatever she asked me to do. I wanted to feel the warmth of her arms around my back."

On the Labour Day, Warren took her to the fair. Both reached there like lovers.

Susie took admission in the University to study journalism. She joined the debating team. She also became a member of a psychological institution.

In October of 1951, Warren wrote in a letter to his Aunt Dorothy Stahl– "I am having a good time with a girlfriend. I have become pretty close to a local girl. After I receive the go ahead from Uncle Fred and you, I will take the next step. This girl has one shortcoming, she does not understand anything about shares, otherwise she is superb."

Warren was making progress. He had prepared well. Instead of proposing he was gradually getting intimate with her. Susie understood that he had decided about her, even though she could not figure how it happened.

Full of enthusiasm, he rejoined the Dale Carnegie course. Warren said, "They used to reward a pencil if you were able to complete a difficult assignment. In the same week, I won a pencil and proposed to Susie."

After this, Susie wrote a detailed and sorrowful letter to Milton Brown. He was stunned. He knew that Susie used to meet Warren, but he never took their friendship seriously.

Warren went to meet Susie's father to seek his blessings. He was confident that Susie's father would grant the blessing easily. But William Thompson took a lot of time before giving his approval. He started discussing the political situation in the country and cursing the Government's policies. He painted a bleak picture of the country's economy and expressed concern that Warren's plans to trade in the stock market could fail. However, he considered him to be a smart boy and capable of facing any eventuality with courage. So even if such an eventuality occurred and her daughter faced hardship, then he would not blame him.

Warren had by now become used to hearing such talk from his father and Susie's father. So he was not disturbed. He kept listening patiently and waited for him to say 'Yes'. Finally after three hours William Thompson gave him permission to marry his daughter.

In April of the same year, Warren and Susie were married.

□

8
Wealth Creation

'Wealth creation is the outcome of a man's thinking capability.'

—Ayn Rand

If you had invested 10,000 dollars in 1956, the year in which Warren Buffett had started investing then today, you would have been worth 350 million dollars.

Warren's success is significant in many ways, because he did not create wealth by patenting a product, or by setting up an industry, or by setting up a retail operation nor by starting his own business. The assets which he used can be easily applied in this capitalist world by everyone– following the principles of extraordinary discipline and investment based on value.

Warren has earned 100 billion dollars till now and is still creating wealth. He believes that there is no magic spell for making profit by investing in others business and anyone can create wealth by doing so. For this one must follow the same rules and principles, which Warren has followed in his life. Anyone can earn money like this and save it for his next generation.

Warren's success story seems unreal and one cannot easily believe it. How a person without the support of his family's wealth, without assuming any responsibility in his family's business, without any recommendation or approach from the higher ups, without working for a fat salary can generate so much wealth and also give most of it towards philanthropy.

It is easy to become rich: by being born in a rich family, by marrying a wealthy a woman or by winning lottery. But becoming rightfully rich is the one tested by Warren-managing your own business and managing it by spending less than your earnings. Like Warren did, you can also convert your dreams of becoming rich into reality by investing in part of others business through the share market. By learning the tricks of investing and management, you can even take controlling stake in that company.

Warren's billions made him the richest man in the world. But he also generated lots of wealth for his partners and shareholders. He generated two dollars for them, for every dollar he generated for himself, his family's four foundations.

By investing over long periods of time, the manner in which he created wealth for himself and others is not really surprising. He strictly followed his principles and became wealthy. Even though, it took him several decades to do so.

First in the middle of sixties, Warren along with his partners started buying shares of a textile mill named Berkshire Hathaway. By 1965, he bought most of its shares for 20 million dollars and took management control of the mill. In 1967, the turnover of the mill was 39 million dollars. In the next four decades by investing his capital he generated 100 billion dollars, he only had to borrow a minor amount.

Extraordinary Capability for Creation of Wealth

In all probability the American writer, poet and philosopher Ralph Waldo Emerson has rightly said that–

"Man is born to become rich and attain prosperity by a mix of his qualities, ideas and nature. Wealth is a product of your mind. To play this game you must learn to be polite, intelligent, swift-footed and patient."

Warren was not born rich but from the very beginning, he had the extraordinary capability to create wealth. All through his life the huge wealth which he created and donated for the welfare of mankind is a result of application of his mental capabilities. He is a polite, intelligent, decisive and a patient person. This amazing story is of a person who started with his hard earned capital and became the richest man in the world in the capitalist system by incessantly using his capabilities appropriately. The wealth which he created is more than the GDP of Iraq, Ethiopia, Costa Rica, Cuba, North Korea and Yemen put together.

Warren was born on 30th August, 1930 in Omaha, a city in Nebraska. Howard Buffett was his father and Leela Stahl Buffett his mother. Jokingly he said that, "He was conceived in his mother's womb in 1929, when the stock market had crashed; because his share broker father had no other work. At that time the senseless behaviour of the investors, is fully registered in my DNA."

Warren often says that being born a white man and an American is his good fortune. He was born in a democratic and capitalist society, where there were immense opportunities for personal growth. If he was born a hundred years earlier or born in a third world country or he had to any other job than investing, then it would not have been possible for him to attain such prosperity. More than 30 books have been written on him, on account of his extraordinary success. From the very beginning he had an uncommon capability to value companies. In addition the time period, in which he was born, was favourable for the economy to expand and capitalism was at its peak. It is equally fortunate that he was born in America where only

2 per cent of the world's population lives; yet has 50 per cent of the world's wealth and has the biggest companies, which has the political and constitutional set up which treats all the professions including investment capabilities equally and had recorded a seven-fold increase in the standard of living in a century.

Warren's friends and Microsoft's creator teased him saying that had he been born a few centuries earlier and did not possess hearing and running capabilities then he would have been gobbled by a wild animal. Or had he been born a woman at a time, when there were a lot of restrictions on women then he would have become a housewife, teacher, secretary or nurse instead of becoming an investor.

Warren's father used to run a stock broking company in Omaha and later became a Congressman from Nebraska. This background also helped to groom Warren's fate. Even though his father did not bestow any money to him because he knew that Warren did not need any ancestral property. His father bestowed him with interest for shares, self-confidence to be independent, high moral standards and developed his political outlook. With the help of all these qualities Warren always succeeded. His father also gave him freedom to form his own opinions. That is why Warren supported his father's opposition party. Both were restless, but Warren's father had a serious disposition whereas Warren was jovial.

20 Per cent Profit at the Age of Six

Warren's grandfather used to run a grocery store, 'Buffett and Son', in Omaha. Being business-minded was in Warren's blood and at the age of six he proved it. He bought pack of 6 cokes for 25 cents from his grandfather's store and sold them separately for a nickel each and earned 20 per cent profit. Thus Warren laid the foundation of being industrious in his future life. At a time when the other children roamed around on the streets in summer evenings, at that time this six year old industrious child was selling coke bottles from door-to-door and learning the art of making money.

From the early years, Warren was interested in arithmetic, numbers, money and coins. His sister told that in his childhood, Warren used to move around with a metal money changer belt. Warren never required a calculator or a computer to solve mathematical problems. From childhood to the present-day, Warren has been continuously involved in making and growing money.

At the age of 8, Warren started reading books on making money and business. '1000 ways to earn 1000 dollars', was his favourite book in the beginning. He read the book several times. By the time he was 10 years old, the billionaire of the future, had read dozens of books on investment, finance, stock market in Omaha's local library. Warren had a sharp memory and he was very good at articulating what he had learnt. He was a wizard with numbers. That is why during his school days, he was promoted by two classes.

His first experience of the stock market was noting down the prices of shares on a blackboard in his father's stock broking office. That is how the prices of shares were displayed before the advent of the electronic display ticker tape and it was called 'marking the board'.

It was while noting down the prices of shares on the blackboard, in June 1942 at the age of eleven, Warren bought his first lot of shares. He bought 6 shares of a company called 'Cities Service Preferred'. He had bought 3 shares in his name and 3 shares in the name of his elder sister Doris. Each share had cost him 38 dollars. So it can be assumed that his personal capital was a little more than 100 dollars at that time. The price of the shares dropped to 27 dollars rapidly, but after some time it increased to 40 dollars. At that time he sold his shares. But from this experience he learnt an important lifelong lesson. Soon after he sold the shares, its price rose to 200 dollars. Possibly at that time he did not realize the error of selling too soon, based on the market price, rather than at its intrinsic value; in his future life he adopted the solid fundamentals of investing.

At the age of 13, displaying exceptional curiosity for learning, Warren had made up his mind to become an investor in the stock market. As a matter of fact he had told a friend of his family that he would become a millionaire by the age of 30. He had also told his father's business partner's wife Mary Falk, while having soup, that if did not become a millionaire, then he would jump from the tallest structure of Omaha.

First Business at the Age of 14

When his father was elected Congressman then Warren had to move to Washington from Omaha to be with his family. There he started studying in high school. He was not very happy to be in the country's capital and he missed Omaha, his birth town. Warren displayed his love and attachment for his birth place all through his life.

At the age of 14 Warren was industrious and ambitious. He started delivering 500 copies of 'Washington Post' newspaper in five localities. He started earning 175 dollars a month.

Like selling coke during his childhood proved to be useful later in life, distributing newspapers also proved to be extremely useful. Later he became the largest shareholder in the newspaper, which he used to distribute in his teens.

Warren's also used to do business of selling used golf balls. For it he took help of his several neighbourhood friends. At the age of 14, he bought 40 acres of farmland in Nebraska for 1200 dollars, which he had saved by delivering newspapers and other activities. He leased out the land to a farmer. This investment was the first sign that he was a determined and self-confident youth, who had become capable of taking firm business decisions, like grown-ups. By investing in the farmland in his early years he expressed his deep-rooted affection for his home state Nebraska. Warren maintained this affection all through his life.

The beauty of this real estate deal was that he did not have to take care of it himself. Even in the later years, Warren did not think that it was necessary for him to visit the head-quarters or the offices of the companies in which he held controlling stakes.

While studying in high school, he bought a used pinball machine for only 25 dollars along with his friend Donald Danly. The original cost of this machine was 300 dollars. He had learnt the art of buying a thing worth one dollar for less than 10 cents in his teens itself. In the later years also he displayed this acumen on several occasions. Both the friend's named the company 'Wilson Coin Operated Machine Company', inspired by their school's name. In front of their customers they posed as if they were the employees of the company and Wilson was the owner. They installed the machine at a barber's saloon.

They earned 5 cents per game and the first week's earning was 4 dollars, which could be called a confidence building return on their investment. When the other barber's asked Warren and Donald to install new machines, they would assure them that they will talk to their owner. They would come back and say that Wilson did not want to buy new machines and only wanted to operate used machines. In this manner they bought 7 used machines and by installing at different barber's shops started earning 50 dollars per week. Next year they sold their business to a War Veteran for 1200 dollars. This experience also helped Warren in the later years. After four decades Warren's company, Berkshire Hathaway became the biggest share-holder, in the world's largest vending machines operator 'Coca Cola'.

Even today on Warren's auto license plate holder, in memory of his teen's business 'Wilson Coin Operated Machine Company' insignia is displayed. It was presented to him by a shareholder.

Warren completed his high school studies at the age of sixteen. At that time he had savings of 6,000 dollars, earned by him. By following the principle of spending less than the earnings, he was living a simple life. By then he had read more than 100 books concerning business. Even today, he is an avid reader and believes in reading a complete book in a day. There was also a time in his life when he read 5 books in a day. He can read 5 times faster than an average reader. He has the same capacity to study the balance sheets of companies; 5 times faster than an average investor. He maintains record of the relevant data also.

The record in his high school year book shows that he was a very good student of mathematics and following the footsteps of his father, he was going to become a stock broker in the future. His father was paying for his college fees and creating an atmosphere for him to save and invest.

College Study: Beginning of Investment On Value-Based Principle

Initially Warren had taken admission in Pennsylvania University but later he moved to Nebraska University and from there obtained his Bachelor of Science degree in Economics in 1950. Warren had a special attachment for Lincoln-based Nebraska University as his parents had fallen in love in its campus. Earlier Warren had read Benjamin Graham's book 'Intelligent Investor' and had been quite impressed by it. Graham later became his Professor, employer and lifelong mentor.

While reading Graham's book Warren discovered the basic principle of investing. The book had highlighted the concept of 'value investing'. It said that the best investment was one which was done by the buyer without being influenced by emotion, fear, rumour or movement of the market but done with due consideration based on value.

Warren had saved 9800 dollars at the age of 19. He applied for admission in Harvard Business School for graduation in Economics but his application was rejected as he was under aged. He was bit disappointed, but another golden opportunity was awaiting him in Columbia. He had heard that Benjamin Graham the author of 'Intelligent Investor', was teaching in Columbia. Warren took admission in Columbia to fulfil his longing to be in the proximity of Graham. David Dodd, who was a famous economist, was also teaching there. Together they had written a 735 pages book on 'Security Analysis'. Warren had been advocating to everyone who wished to operate in the stock market to read this book. The formula to work out the true value of a company had been given in the book.

At the age of 21, in 1951, Warren came to know that Graham was working as the CEO of G.E.I.C.O. Auto Insurance. Warren realized that if a person like Graham was associated with this business, then he could get an excellent opportunity to learn the cues for investing under his guidance. Warren proceeded to Washington D.C. from New York by train on a Saturday. He reached the auto insurance company's headquarters and obtained information regarding the company from an Officer of the company. Evidently the learning of the auto insurance business came in handy in the latter years, when his company bought the full ownership of the auto insurance company.

One of the important principles of Warren's is that all information about the company must be gathered before investing so that its true valuation can be assessed. How does the company make money, what is its stability, what are its shortcomings, what are its growth potential, what is the strength of its competitor's, how effective is its management and how honest it is, etc. complete information on all such parameters must be obtained.

His visit to the headquarters of G.E.I.C.O. helped him to understand several such factors. Based on this information, Warren invested in G.E.I.C.O. shares. Next year he was attracted by a new share, so he sold these shares for 15,259 dollars and invested in a new company's shares.

Warren had learnt so much about G.E.I.C.O. that merely at the age of 21 he wrote a research report titled 'The share which I like most', for a magazine called 'The Commercial and Financial Chronicle'. On the basis of his research he found out that G.E.I.C.O. was earning 5 times profit as compared to its competitors because they were selling directly without the help of agents. He was fully aware of the details of this company. So in 1976, through Berkshire Hathaway, he bought one third of the auto insurance company's shares for 45.7 million dollars. Later he bought more shares and increased the shareholding to 50 per cent. In 1995 he bought rest of the 50 per cent shares for 2.3 billion dollars and gained complete ownership. He thus added another company to his list of companies which were continuously earning profit.

In 1951, Warren got his graduation degree in economics. Warren wanted to work in Wall Street, but his father Howard Buffett and Graham asked him not to do so. These two influential persons in Warren's life had seen the depression and were fully aware of the ups and downs of the share market. Both of them advised the young and ambitious graduate to get a secured job in a reputed company. Both believed that there was a lot of uncertainty in share prices in the share market. Warren did not follow the advice.

Warren proposed Graham that he would work for him as a share researcher and analyst for free but Graham rejected the proposal. Even though Warren was the only student to whom Graham had graded with A+ for share analysis. Warren jokingly said that after receiving the proposal, The Honourable Professor, quickly did cost-benefit analysis and concluded that in spite of the fact that Warren was going to work for free, the trade would not be profitable. However, the real reason was that it was the policy of Graham-Neumann partnership to employ Jews only. The Jews were not given jobs on Wall Street and so Graham tried to balance the scales by giving opportunities to Jews. Therefore, Warren returned to Omaha and started getting close to his sister's college classmate Susan Thompson.

Choice of the Right Guides and Good Practices

Warren has been telling students, "If you tell me who is your ideal person, then I will tell you the type of person you are. Initially the pressure of the shackles of habit is slight, but later it becomes so overwhelming that it becomes impossible to release it". In other words, the manner in which your leader explains to you, your habits also define you.

To motivate the students Warren used to say, "Choose such a classmate to whom you would like to give 10 per cent of your income in the future. Then the students did not choose the most bright, best sportsman or the most handsome classmate. They used to choose classmates with good habits, who guided you correctly, who observed values and ideals. There is nothing better than honesty and the whole world trusts such a person."

He used to say– "Whomsoever they considered to be their ideal, observed the good qualities of his character and keep noting them down. Continue this practice. As you continue the practice, it will also start changing your mental visualization. When you make the list of habits which you like then you will also like to develop those habits yourself. You can never build your character by trying only once in your life time; nor can you build it by having prerogative, status or wealth. You can build a strong character by observing minute details of your daily activities."

At an age when most of the youngsters considered sports stars and film actors as their ideals, Warren guided by his inner motivation and wisdom had chosen his father and Graham to be his mentors. Instead of considering the famous basketball player Jo DiMaggio or the sensational singer Elvis Presley as his ideals, Warren had chosen a stock broker-cum-state leader and a Professor-cum-teacher of value-based investment as his ideals. Under their guidance he developed the skills of value investing, decision-making and learnt important principles and policies.

Every person can willfully choose his own guide and habits. Our habits define our character. The good thing is that we can change our habits. It is easy to change our habits when we are young. Possibly for this reason, Warren used to like talking to students and motivating them. Warren became a role model for thousands of investors, businessmen, managers and his competitors by choosing the right mentors, achieving extraordinary success and developing disciplinary habits.

Beginning Career As a Stock Broker

Warren started working as a stock broker in his father's company Buffett-Falk Company. He also joined the evening classes in Omaha University. His subject was, Principles of investing. The other students were double his age. Warren was not focusing only on achieving financial success. In 1952, he married his sister's friend Susan. He moved to a small rented apartment. Its rent was 65 dollars a month. After one year, his first child was born. When he had gone for his honeymoon to California by road, he had carried with him Graham's book 'Security Analysis', to study it again, in the back seat of his car.

While working for his father, Warren was in constant touch with Graham. He kept sending him his research papers on stocks and stock picks, which also included his research on G.E.I.C.O. Auto Insurance. In 1954, Graham invited Warren to work in the Company's headquarters. His starting salary was 12,000 dollars a year. It was slightly less than the 13,800 dollars average salary of the premier baseball league players but much more than the 5,000 dollars salary of a New York school teacher. After two years, Graham decided to retire and he dissolved his partnership.

After working with Graham for two years, Warren was now ready to start his own investment partnership in his home town. Six years back when he had completed his college education his saving was 9,800 dollars, which had now grown to 1,40,000 dollars. He would spend sparingly and continued value-investing. A 26 year old youth taking such wise decisions used to astonish every one.

The Beginning of Investment Partnership

Warren returned to Omaha from New York and started a small Investment Partnership Company. He made only his family members and friends as partners. There were only 7 partners in this business, which he operated from his home, who had invested a total sum of 1,05,000 dollars. Warren had invested only 700 dollars. Without having a formal office or Secretary, without using a calculator, in the next 13 years Warren's company earned 29.50 per cent average profit and did not make loss even in a single year. Warren's eldest child and only daughter Susan says that when she was young she used to think that her father did home alarms business because he used to work from home and used to work as a Security Analyst.

In 1957, when Warren's wife was about to deliver their third child, he bought a 5 bedroom stucco house for 31,500 dollars on Farnam Street in Omaha. He had spent 10 per cent of his total wealth on the purchase. He stays in the same house even today. This investment shows glimpse of the future billionaire's adherence to the fundamental principles of investment. His principle has been to save, invest and spend only 10 per cent of your wealth; whereas most people deposit their entire savings towards down payment for buying a house and for the next 20 years continue to pay the instalments and remain as the banks debtors. Warren had given another message that after buying a house, one must not leave it and definitely not sell it at any price. With his intention to never sell his house, Warren will leave his house and his company Berkshire Hathaway as it is, after him.

Warren has impressed his shareholders with such principles and his life's philosophy. Such shareholders who bought the shares at the issue price of 17 dollars, have continued to be associated with his company for more than 27 years. Warren has been winning the faith of his shareholders by his exceptional policies and have decided on retaining their relationship with his company.

When Warren achieved the target of becoming a millionaire by the age of 30, nobody was surprised. By 1962 Warren's company which at start valued at 10,500 dollars was worth 7.2 million dollars. He opened his office in a tall building on Farnam Street itself, where he works even today with handful of employees. The office is close to his house.

In the beginning of the 60's, while researching, he identified a textile manufacturing company named Berkshire Hathaway based in New Bedford, Massachusetts. Before investing, he would undertake thorough research for selecting the right company. He started buying shares of this company at 7 dollars a share, which was lower than its value of 17 dollars a share. The company had a small debt. For investing in this company, he applied the principle of value-investing. By 1963, Warren's partnership company had become the largest shareholder in Berkshire Hathaway.

Building A Stock Portfolio

In 1965 after meeting Walt Disney personally, Warren started investing in Walt Disney Company. He had taken the decision to invest in this company after a lot of analysis as he had done before investing in G.E.I.C.O. Later, he developed so much expertise that he started investing without meeting the management of the company or without visiting the company and just by studying the balance sheet of the company. Warren bought Disney's 5 per cent shares for 4 million dollars. It was a debt free company. If he had 80 million dollars he would have bought the entire company. Today it would have been worth more than 40 billion dollars.

He sold it for 6 million dollars a year later. If Warren had retained his initial investment today, it would have been worth 7 to 12 billion dollars (including the dividends and spin-offs). It seems amazing that a company which totally valued at 80 million dollars at that time, today in that amount only a roller coaster can be bought for its entertainment park. When warren had invested in the company, Disney had spent 17 million dollars to develop its entertainment park and had produced approximately 200 animated films. So if Warren or anyone else had researched the company, it would not have been difficult to find out that the company's true value was much higher. Today, if Warren were to invest in this company, considering its true value, he would prefer to buyout the company provided he had sufficient funds to do so.

In the same year, in the board meeting, Warren took control of Berkshire Hathaway. He appointed Ken Chase as the CEO to manage the textile business of the company. Later this company became his holding and investment company. This company had a working capital of 19 dollars per share, whereas Warren had bought the shares at the rate of 14.86 dollars per share. This price did not include the fixed assets (building and machinery), of the company. At the age of 36, Warren's personal wealth had become 5 million dollars and few years later it became 10 million dollars. His investment partnership company's wealth had become 65 million dollars. It not less than a miracle that at the age of 38 in 1968 Warren's investment partnership company was earning 40 million dollars every year and it was valued at 104 million dollars.

In 1969, the year after his most successful year, he closed his investment partnership and distributed the several hundred million dollars of portfolio to all the partners. He took this decision after he realized that in the changing circumstances, the opportunities based on value investing had become fewer, whereas the shareholders expectations were skyrocketing. The assets which he distributed to the shareholders also included the shares of Berkshire Hathaway. At that time at the age of 39, his personal share holding was worth 25 million dollars and he owned 50 per cent of Berkshire Hathaway.

At this time, he also started writing an annual letter to his shareholders, which later become a very popular communication. Seeing his exceptional ability for creation of wealth, the people wanted to know what was going on in his mind. Through his annual letter, he used to share information about his company and the share market in a very easy to understand language. Warren always used to consider his shareholders as his partners and maintained communication with them through his annual letter.

Through this letter he used to explain the fundamentals of investing and his life's philosophy and has been attracting new investors.

There was another turning point in his life, when in addition to making money through his partnership; he started creating wealth by investing in public limited companies.

In that year, when his textile company earned a profit of 45,000 dollars, his investments in insurance, banking other businesses earned more than 10 times, an amount of 4.7 million dollars. Warren started experimenting with new ways to create wealth. He started using the profits from his insurance and operating company to buy other businesses. Thus he started creating wealth much faster and kept continuously advancing towards the peak of his success.

Warren's investment strategy could be understood thus–Berkshire was investing in businesses, who were earning profit and reinvesting in such companies, who delivered a higher profit. Warren used to exercise his say in the operations of the companies in his portfolio and their management. Warren had invested 400 million dollars in the insurance sector which he used for other sectors and kept on increasing the profits. People started calling Berkshire 'Capital Allocating Machine'.

In 1973, when the share market started showing sign of dipping, Berkshire bought shares of 'Washington Post' and became its largest shareholder. Thirty years earlier, Warren used to sell this newspaper. Even today, Warren holds this investment and earns 9 million dollars in dividends every year. This amount was equivalent to the principal amount which he had invested.

After a year in 1974, when the share market entered the bear phase, on account of the global oil crisis, he lost half of his wealth. Later in 1974, when the markets recovered, Berkshire's share rose to 290 dollars and it was worth 140 million dollars. Even at that time he was drawing an annual salary of only 50,000 dollars. He was against any kind of wasteful expenditure.

In the next 4 years, based on value-investing and with the contribution from his insurance and other companies, Berkshire's corporate stock portfolio had amassed wealth of 1.3 billion dollars. In the beginning of 1983 Berkshire's share was quoting at 775 dollars per share, which increased to 1,300 dollars per share during that year itself. At that time Warren's personal stake was worth 420 million dollars and he was fast approaching towards becoming a billionaire. 'Forbes Magazine' added his name in the world's richest persons' list.

In 1985, Warren closed down Berkshire's textile business on account of global competition due to cheaper labour. At one time it was Berkshire Hathaway's core business which had now become insignificant. After one year Berkshire's shares price increased to over 3000 dollars and Warren became a billionaire.

In 1988, Warren made up his mind to initiate his childhood business from a new perspective. At the age of 58 year, Warren started buying Coca Cola Company's shares like an obsessed man. He bought 8 per cent shares of the company for 1 billion dollars and became the largest shareholder. In 1936, when he was 6 years old he had made 20 per cent profit by selling coke. Since childhood Warren's fascination for soft drinks business persisted. In 1988 Coca Cola Company was buying back its shares and Warren was impressed by its managing capabilities. He was buying shares at the price of 5 dollars a share. Compared to technology business, he understood Coca Cola as product much better and knew very well how profits could be generated from this product. The product had been established in the world's markets. He knew that like his other investments, his investment in Coca Cola would yield profits continuously.

Before investing in the company, he had not contacted anyone in the company to ascertain the facts. He had researched the information available to the general public for this purpose. He did not think that it was wise to approach the management because at that time the company was buying back its own shares and believing this to be an opportune signal for investing. He decided to buy as many shares as possible. He bought 200 million shares of Coke. At first the Coke's management was worried about this unexpected buying but when they came to that Warren had bought the shares, their fears were allayed. They were worried because the competing companies also make such purchases in an effort to vest control of the company. Warren respected Coke's management and did not wish to exercise his control over them. The Management appointed him on their Board of Directors. Warren still has been regularly cooperating with the company and playing an important role in its growth. His elder son Howard Graham Buffett is a Board Member of, 'Coca Cola Enterprises', its bottling unit.

Coca Cola controls 70 per cent share of the world's soft drinks market. It sells 1.8 billion bottles of soft drinks every day. Warren invested in Coke because he knew that it would be a value-based investment and it would generate profits continuously.

From the very beginning Warren became involved with Coca Cola, Washington Post and G.E.I.C.O. When he grew up he continued his attachment with these companies by buying their shares. He became owner of a textile company also. He invested the profit from it in other businesses and kept on earning profit continuously.

By 1988, Warren had acquired ownership in different businesses. He had started acquiring ownership of 4-5 companies every year and had become a worldwide famed billionaire. People started calling him the 'Saint of Omaha'. Worldwide students of management and business have researched his success story. If he starts showing interest in any company, its share price shoots up. Taking advantage of this phenomenon, many companies have floated rumours of Warren's interest in their company, in a bid to raise the prices of their shares.

Warren achieved an annual return of 29.55 per cent for 13 years through Buffett Partnership and an annual return of 22.6 per cent for 38 years through Berkshire Hathaway. He created new records of achieving success in the 5 decades of his glorious investment career.

Warren increased the valuation of Berkshire Hathaway from 40 million dollars to 66 billion dollars. Warren is most certainly the greatest experimenter of economic value in a free capitalistic society. He is an extraordinarily talented and lucky person. He has practiced with a unique fusion of mathematics and business skills. He achieved extraordinary success by inculcating qualities like patience, discipline, self-confidence, decisive ability, wisdom and independent thinking. Other people may also possess such qualities but it is not easy for everyone to apply them. It becomes very difficult to defend such human qualities, particularly in an economic environment of professionalism and consumerism.

Warren reached the pinnacle of success in an era of expanding capalist economy. At the beginning of the century the Dow Jones Industrial Index's, average was 66, which reached 11,000 in 100 years. One can gauge the extent of growth of capital through this index. However, it is possible to succeed in any economic set up by following Warren's principles. J.P.Morgan had said, "In business, important decisions can only be taken based on a high degree of character." Warren is a living example of this saying. Like Warren, anyone can create immense wealth by not compromising with one's principles and following simple rules of investing.

Value-based Investing Versus Investing Based On Mass Frenzy

Some people differentiate between value-investor and growth-investor. Warren believes that both are linked to each other. The objective of investing is to earn profit in the future by deploying the funds today.

Are you owner of a business or just a seller? To decide this, Warren suggests raising questions from the beginning. Do you track the present and the future earnings of a business or do you assess it based on its price? Is your investment decision based on study and research or are you influenced by others opinion? People who invest considering the value are independent thinkers. Such people do not take the decision to invest based on mass frenzy. They form their own independent opinion by conducting their own research and studying incessantly. They may study the activities of others but never copy them. Such people like to choose their own path. They decide to invest only after assessing their expectations, time period and risk taking capacity.

It has been the common belief that one must invest more in shares when they are young and switch to safer investment avenues as they grow old. They must also consider their age, marital status etc. while investing.

In contrast Warren believes that age should not be a criterion. Whether you buy shares or invest in fixed return instruments, its merit and value-based price should be the basis. He also believes that one must not be scared by the uncertainties of investing. Problems arise when the investor does not have the information or does not know what he is doing.

Comparison of the Market Beliefs Versus Warren's Beliefs

Market beliefs	*Warren's beliefs*
(a) Mass	Individual
(b) Emotional	Wisdom
(c) Price-based	Value-based
(d) Manifold	Focused
(e) Spectator	Owner
(f) Not committed	Loyal
(g) Higher cost and taxes	Lower cost and taxes
(h) Sell	Study
(i) Average 6 months investment	Life-long ownership

From the above table it is easy to understand the difference between the markets and Warren's techniques of investment.

□

9

Warren Buffett's Principles of Investment

In the beginning, Warren learnt the principles of investing, under the guidance of his father and later refined those principles under his mentor Benjamin Graham. Warren's investing principles can be expressed by the following two simple rules–

Rule 1. Never lose money.

Rule 2. Never forget Rule 1.

Warren says that, "An active investor must carry out three jobs everyday– study, research and thinking."

Warren's investments principles can be summarized as follows:

- Know what you have.
- Research before investing.
- Become the owner of the business and not of the share.
- Just do 20 important investments in your life time.
- Resolve to be a long-term investor at the time of buying the share.

All the factors which you will consider before you buy a company must also be considered before you buy its shares.

Initially, Warren used the cigar smoking example to invest, according to which he used to buy old companies. Such companies would be almost at the end of their life cycles. Such companies were left with limited earning opportunities, like the few puff of a cigar. The main example of this is Berkshire Hathaway Textile Mill, which was left with only 20 years or less of operational life.

Thereafter, he moved ahead and started investing in companies which were available at fair price but earned much higher profit. His investment in Gillette Company is an example of this. In 1989 Warren bought shares worth 6 million dollars of this company. Warren's holding company owns 11 per cent of the world's largest razor blade company, valued at 3 billion dollars. He had bought the shares at the price of 6.25 dollars per share which started yielding an annual return of 12 per cent in 14 years. Warren learnt that every night the beard of 2.5 billion people grew. Gillette's has 70 per cent share in the world's razor market.

Warren's advice is to try and buy an uncommon business or share, at the lowest price. He himself has been buying a dollar's worth of property, for only 50 cents.

Warren believes that during one's life time, only 20 important investments must be done. This principle was proposed by his Guru Benjamin Graham. He also believes that it takes 20 years to build one's reputation, but it can be destroyed in a moment. An investor must build his reputation to be successful.

□

10

Women In Warren's Life

At the age of 78, for the first time Warren Buffett shared the intimate aspects of his life with a female writer Alice Schroeder in detail. His official biography "The Snowball: Warren Buffett and the Business of Life; based on this interview was published."

It has been revealed in this book that Warren did not always spend a peaceful and balanced life. He faced emotional upheavals also. He was an emotional and love starved husband. At the same time as a father, he did not give sufficient attention to his children. He avoided people who were likely to criticize him.

Warren considered his four time elected Congressman Father to be his ideal; but had a difficult relationship with his mother. His mother who was considered as a model housewife by the outside world, used to scold the little Warren and his elder sister until they were in tears. Warren told that he did not cry when his mother passed away, though he felt sad. In Warren's words "My mother had her merits also, but her shortcomings kept me aloof from her."

The book highlights the women in Warren's life, who tried to fill his loneliness and gave him emotional happiness. Susan, his wife for 25 years was the most important woman. After marriage they stayed in Omaha with their 3 children. Warren was busy in his work round the clock. Susan knew that Warren expected her to love him and did not like to be criticized. In their social life, they both appeared to be a happy couple, where Warren would often embrace her. But in their personal life, Warren who was busy creating wealth did not have time for his wife. Then Susan used to think of the time when his husband will have 8 to 10 million dollars and will be able to spend time with his family. But Susan failed to understand the fact that at the age of 6, the boy who while selling coke to his neighbours had decided on his objective, it was going to continue without any break. Warren was one day going to become the richest man in the world by creating wealth by following his principles and spending it frugally.

When their children grew up and settled, Susan decided to stay separately and moved to San Francisco. They separated in 1977 but never divorced. Warren and Susan lived separately for 27 years, but they used to talk regularly with each other over phone. Warren had realized his mistake and was also quite hurt by Susan's annoyance. He used to aimlessly walk in the house. He was neither conscious of his food or his clothes. At first Susan thought of returning back to him, then she decided against it and instead sent Astrid Menks who used to work as a hostess in a restaurant to look after him.

Later Warren told, "Susan used to take care of me; Astrid also started taking care of me." Susan died of heart attack in 2004. Warren married Astrid on 30th August, 2006, at the age of 76.

There were other women also in Warren's life, but his attention was primarily focused on expanding his business. One of the other women was Sharon Osberg, who was a bridge player. On her say, Warren had agreed to use the computer. Earlier Warren had refused even his friend Bill Gates to use the computer. Similarly, he became friends with Carol Loomis who was a writer of 'Fortune', magazine. She used to edit his annual letter to the shareholders.

There was a lot of talk on his close relations with Katherine Graham who was the publisher of, 'Washington Post'. Warren had met Katherine Graham when he had invested in the shares of, 'Washington Post'. Through her, he had got the opportunity of meeting and developing relations with society's elite. Warren played an important role in explaining the finer points of the business to Katherine.

□

11

A Turning Point

As Warren became more and more busy with his business trips to New York, Washington, Buffalo and other places, he was becoming more and more distant from his wife Susie. Both were living separate sort of lives. Susie was seriously considering of taking up singing. Musician Neil Sedaka heard her singing in Omaha and suggested to her that she should start singing as a professional. Warren's investment manager and friend Bill Ruane arranged for Susie's audition in Tramp, Ball Room and other night clubs of Manhattan. Warren's New-York based friends were surprised and realized that Susie could sing quite well. According to the reigning singer Rosen Prent, "If she had been a common singer, nobody would have bothered, but she was the wife of a very wealthy man.

After receiving an invitation to participate in a music program in New York, Susie thought of improving her singing and touring different cities. She also entered into an agreement with the talent agency, 'William Morris.'

In the winter of 1977, when Warren was in the process of buying, 'Buffalo Evening News', a music program was being organized for Susie in Omaha's French Cafe. After the conclusion of the program, a party was held at Warren's house, for the guests. After spending a little time in the party, Warren proceeded to his study and Susie kept entertaining the guests. Warren's youngest son Peter later told, "Dad was reading in the study room and Mummy was looking after the guests."

Both of them had become extremely busy, so much so, that in April, 1977 when they were celebrating their weddings Silver Jubilee Anniversary, cartoonist Stan Lipsay drew a cartoon of both of them floating over their anniversary cake.

Both of them had different interests and after the children grew up, Susie felt very lonely in the house. Their family friend and those times well-known artist Kent Bellows believed that Warren's and Susie's married life was a success and referring to their contrasting nature, said that they were an example of how opposites attract each other. Warren often would hide behind a screen like a snail hides in his shell. Even though he would be physically present but his mind would be elsewhere. He would either be reading a book or lost in his thoughts. Socially, he was completely unlike Susie.

Susie had told Bellows, "To be happy, all that Warren needs is a 60 watt bulb and a book," whereas, Susie liked to do lots of things to be happy. She essentially believed in making others happy. She liked to be emotionally involved with people. It was in her nature to live for others and for ages she had been sacrificing her body and soul for Warren's happiness.

Her daughter says, "Mummy went through lot of hardships to help Dad. She made sure that Dad did not face any difficulties in carrying out his work. Dad was an introvert and was always dedicated towards his work. He has been doing the same type of work."

While her son Peter says, "Mummy underwent a lot of hardships to keep others happy. It was only very late in the evening, when she had some time for herself, she used to listen to music."

In an exclusive interview with, 'Omaha World Herald', on her singing career, Susie had praised Warren for fully helping her in her singing career. The article based on this interview was published two days before their marriage's silver jubilee anniversary. On her relationships, Susie had told that she was madly in love with another boy but heeding to her father's advice, she had chosen Warren as her life partner and found out that he was an extraordinary person. In the interview, she never mentioned whether she fell in love with Warren after her marriage nor did she express her pain which she felt after her separation from Milton Brown. Even 25 years after her marriage, she used to remember Milton Brown and used to wonder about her life, if she been married to Milton Brown instead of Warren. At that time Milton had become a successful grain broker in Des Moines.

At that time both of them were feeling pangs of loneliness. Their daughter was married and was working in a company called Century 21 in Irvin, California. She was also studying in college. Howard had left his college studies from Augustana College in Sioux Falls, South Dakota. He was starting his own business by setting up a company near Omaha. To buy the equipment, he was using his shares in Berkshire Hathaway. Peter had taken admission in Stanford University.

In September 1977, Susie performed in Omaha's famous Music Theatre Orpheum. Artists like L. Johnson and Barbara Stanczak used to perform in this theatre, in the 30s. During the program Susie performed in a confident manner in front of her hometown audience and won their hearts. Ecstatically addressing the audience she said, "It feels as if we are madly in love."

After a few days of this event, 45 year old Susie decided to part ways with her husband Warren. She left Warren's house on Farnam Street in Omaha and moved to San Francisco, where she started living in a rented apartment. She also informed her children about this. While Howard was shocked, Peter was not much surprised. Susie told her children that she was not legally separating from Warren, but she wanted to lead her life as she wished.

Susie's leaving was like a deadly blow for Warren, the suffering of which could not be expressed in words. Warren was shocked and stunned. He could not understand the reason why Susie left him. She was like a shield for him who used to protect him from calamities and difficulties; she used to maintain the right ambience in the house so that he could focus on his work. With her love and affection, she used to generate a feeling of warmth in the house and she used to take care of even his minor needs with her kind heart. Warren had told his elder sister, "Susie for me is like the rain and sunshine for my garden."

Left alone, Warren could not fathom the reason as to why Susie left him. While talking to Susie over phone he started crying bitterly. Susie comforted him sympathetically and told him that she had not broken her relationship with him but had only decided to stay separately due to the compulsions of her circumstances. They could still talk over the phone, travel together and even spend their holidays together at New York and their seaside Resort at Laguna. She continued her emotional chatting with Warren over phone. She allayed his fears by saying that they were still husband and wife; but the essence of her response was that we both have separate needs.

After Susie left him, Warren's daughter Susie Jr. came to stay with him for a few weeks. She found that her father was in a state of shock and was feeling helpless. Susie Jr. tried to console her father. Incidentally, she was also trying to get out of her marriage. She tried to dispel the loneliness in the house and assumed all the household responsibilities skillfully. She started feeding her father proper food instead of popcorn and made sure that he was dressed decently. Warren was very much impressed by his daughter's adeptness. He could not believe that she easily completed ironing of the clothes in the afternoon. Susie Jr. later told that Dad did not talk much about Mom.

"Dad was taking his time to become stable. I only remember that Dad used to keep reading, sitting in a chair and would talk about ironing of clothes. I even told him that nothing had changed. However, if you still expect being welcomed by her, the moment the door opens then it means that you still feel her presence in the house".

Warren's relations and friends who always used to praise the Warren family were surprised on Susie's departure and were also hurt. But it was not as if Warren and Susie were shattered by the separation. Even though Susie was in California, they used to talk everyday over the phone. During Christmas, they would meet along with their two children at their Laguna Beach House. During winter, Warren and Susie would spend two weeks together in New York.

The situation was becoming normal. His daughter told, "Dad had started realizing that his life had not undergone a major upheaval. In fact he had been shaken by the sudden change. He even thought of moving to Southern California, where most of his relations were settled; but he could not implement his decision. One of the reasons was that he could not manage his affairs without his longtime and loyal Secretary Gladys Kessler. Secondly, he did not want to change his daily routine. He did not want to leave his established set up and start afresh."

On the other hand, Susie was living a carefree life. Her apartment was decorated like a teenager's room. All the modern gadgets had been provided. Living alone, she tasted the joyous feeling of freedom, after a long period of time. To gain this type of freedom, she had to wait for her middle-age. There were some aspects of her personal life which she did not wish to share with Warren; she knew that Warren could not handle those aspects. The family members knew, as well as, understood that Susie had some personal needs and they could not overlook them. The family members tried to build a shield around Warren so that he could continue his work unhindered. The family members had extended such support to Warren earlier also. His younger sister Roberta even said, "We all have been concerned about Warren, I don't know how it all started, but from the very early stage the thinking has been like that."

Susie had been emotionally protecting Warren. Even while living separately she was taking care of Warren in her own style. She had the art of making new friends, at the same time; she remained worried about taking care of her husband's smallest needs. She requested several women of Omaha to take care of her husband for cinema shows and to restaurants for eating outside. One of them was Astrid Menks. Thirty one year old Astrid used to work in Omaha's French Café as a waitress. Astrid started making different types of dishes for Warren and started looking after him. Susan also encouraged her.

Astrid was much better than Warren in socializing with different groups. The rural type of locality of Market District where she used to live was undergoing changes and was getting influenced by modernization. Astrid was born in Latvia and had moved to Omaha when she was a child. Her mother had passed away when she was very young. Her father, who used to work as a waiter, had put his children in an orphanage. In simple terms Astrid was a spirited teenager. She was diplomatic and hard working. She would appear mod and attractive even in second hand attire. Her innocent round face would remind of her origins. In winter, braving the icy winds, wearing a fur coat when she used to stroll around the roads of Omaha with a red dog she seemed to appear like a character from a detective novel.

Astrid was fully familiar with Omaha's well-known people from the respected class. One of Warren's nephew Tom Rogers used to stay above the French Café. He later told, "When it started snowing and people felt the chill, in any case Omaha's residents were very spiritualistic about the snow then Astrid used to arrange dinner for Warren with enthusiasm." She wanted to be useful and helpful to others, but liked to remain in the background. When Susie had sung in the French Café then Astrid had brought tea for her. She was very alert in welcoming the guests and was always courteous.

Astrid moved in with Warren within a year of Susie's departure. Warren's son Howard was upset with this move. The others were surprised by the turn of the events. Astrid's friend from the second-hand things shop Kent Bellows an artist was astonished that she had moved with the richest man in town.

Bellow's asked Astrid, "What is cooking between you and Warren? Are you...."

It was rumoured that Warren had employed her as a cook; but in reality both of them had developed marital like relationship. Temperamentally both of them were made for each other. Both of them believed in leading a cheerful and simple life. When Warren would be busy with his stock investing then Astrid would go around the second-hand stuff sellers searching for bargains or negotiate for buying Pepsi-Cola in the Super Market. When Warren was busy in his study, she would relax in the garden. Astrid liked to stay in the house and she had relieved Warren from all the household responsibilities. Whenever Peter would arrive by a late night train, she used to go to the station to pick him up.

Possibly after having experienced loneliness herself, she did not regret her dedication in looking after Warren.

She was serving Warren without any complaint whatsoever. The arrangement between the two of them was curious. Astrid had got a home and a male companion. Warren had got a female companion and a woman to look after his home. From the day she moved into the house, Astrid knew that Warren was not going to marry her because he was still attached to Susie. Astrid had decorated Warren's house, but when Susie was in town then she would watch him going to meet her in ironed clothes.

In the beginning when Warren went out of town to meet Susie, Astrid would also travel out of Omaha, instead of staying alone in the house. But after some time she did not feel any inconvenience, also her relationship with his family members had eased. She also managed to establish pleasant relations with Susie. When Susie used to come to Omaha she would take Astrid out with her for lunch. Susie did not stay in the Farnam street house. During the AGM of Berkshire Hathaway, when people saw Susie and Astrid sitting together there were many gossip talks. At that time Warren was sitting on the dais.

The relationship between the three persons had got into a curious rhythm. Astrid would take care of Warren in his day-to-day life, whereas Susie would accompany him outside Omaha. They would meet their old friends in New York and California together. They would also attend the official functions together.

For the outside world their deep love for each other was still intact. Lodge Retailer Jo Rosenfeld used to often meet Warren and Susie in California. He later told, "They both appeared to be a happy couple."

Susie Jr. told that the basic relationship between her mother and father was the same as it was earlier. Peter told that even though they were staying 1500 miles apart, their hearts were still united.

Howard Neumann, who was the son of Benjamin Graham's partner Neumann, had mocked about Warren's relationship with two women. But Warren was fully aware of his life's reality. Both the women in his life had a distinct and specific place. It seemed as if everything was predestined. There was a lot of difference between the personalities of Susie and Astrid. Neither were they acting their roles nor could they exchange their roles. Even though it was difficult for Warren's friends to understand their triangular relationship, they had started accepting the relationship.

The question which arises is whether Warren was content with his married life? Peter says that at the time of marriage not much attention was paid on whether Mummy had given her consent for marriage or not, though Warren denies it. Or was he weaving new relations so that he could carry on his work unhindered. Even though his friends found the new set up strange, but Warren was comfortable with the changed circumstances and was able to carry out his work. The mental support which he used to seek, he was able to secure from Susie in spite of the distance between them. Even in his youth, he used to return to Omaha to seek mental support. He was able to save himself from the pain of divorce due to the new circumstances. He was never provoked to take any revengeful action due to frustration from it. He had accepted the change of the circumstances.

He had told a reporter, "I love my life. I have woven my life in a manner which allows me to carry out the work which I enjoy the most." He was not bothered with what people thought about him nor did he have any qualms about seeking social approval. He did not feel it necessary to defend his actions. His only comment had been that none of the three persons had any problem on account of the triangular relationship.

"When you are close to a person, then there can be no problem in understanding the mutual feelings."

Warren would forcefully tell his friends that it was Susie who has chosen Astrid for him. After Astrid had moved in with Warren, his old friend, with whom he had operated the pinball machines Donald Denali toured Omaha and stayed with him. He was surprised to see Astrid and could not understand their relationship, till later in the night when he saw Warren and Astrid going to the same bedroom. Warren told that Susie and Astrid were friends. Later Denali told, "I think this statement was important for Warren. He was trying to explain that he himself had not taken any wrong decision."

On the other hand, Peter believed that the one year which his father spent without Susie had been extremely tortuous for him.

"Everything appeared desolate to him and he was in grief." A female friend of the family told that Warren felt quite lonely. But he was also trying to cope with it courageously. Except for people who were close to him, nobody else knew about his mental agony. According to Peter, sometimes Warren was not even conscious of his mental state. He kept himself busy with his work and was trying to instinctively accept the changed plan, which had happened in his life.

When he was young, he had faced a similar turmoil. Warren had to move to Washington from Omaha against his wishes. To overcome it, he had immersed himself body and soul in the job of delivering newspapers. Now he owns several of those newspapers but he still retained the same sense of anxiety which he felt when he was young. He could not rise early even though there were piles of papers waiting for his attention in the office. He used to talk loudly over phone so that the person on the other side would not get any inkling of his pain. But in the company of the two women, his will power was becoming stronger.

According to his old friend Rosenfeld, "I never saw Warren dispirited. He was always involved with Berkshire."

Saved from being involved in the day-to-day personal affairs, Warren started experiencing some kind of creative energy. In the late 70s, Warren in his own inimitable style took several important investment decisions. Delighted by the fall in the share market, he was investing funds from Berkshire Insurance Company in shares. Some of the leading companies were– Amerada Hess Corporation, American Broadcasting Corporation, General Foods, G.E.I.C.O., Night Riders Newspapers, Media General, Safeco Auto Insurance, F.W. Woolworth etc.

During that time it was said that, if there was rumour of Warren buying shares of any company, its price used to rise by 10 per cent. General Foods shares price was falling. Broker Earl Roper says, "Warren would not disclose what he was going to buy. He would wait patiently for the price to dip and then start buying."

He wanted to ink the story of his progress, but from the time of formation of the partnership firm till now, he had been silent. He started writing articles for business magazines. He also expressed his views in Berkshire Hathaway's annual report. Every year he started writing a letter to the shareholders of Berkshire Hathaway expressing openly his views on investing, management and finance.

It is not definite as to when he started penning his views. But when a collection of his letters was published, the first letter pertained to the year 1977, which was written in the beginning of 1978. Coincidently, it was the time when Susie had already left his house to live separately. In this letter he had discussed his views on several fundamental issues but it is doubtful if many people read it. He had told that before buying the shares of a company, he used to investigate the company as if he was buying the company itself. He used to be on the lookout of such companies of which he understood the working and business; its management was honest and capable. He also paid particular attention on its potential in the future. Then he would wait for buying the shares at the lowest possible price. He never invested for short-term gains.

Warren's approach and his investment strategy for buying shares in the 70s created a sensation on Wall Street. The type of shares which Warren considered ideal for investing were available; but nobody was prepared to buy them. In the summer of 1970. Dow Jones Index fell even below the level of 1969. In the middle of 70s the country's economic condition seemed precarious and all the headlines in the newspapers reflected pessimism. The Dollar was weakening against the Mark and Yen. The fundamentalist forces were on the rampage. The energy crisis had started biting. The feeling of despair was spreading in the country. Nixon's ignominious rule had come to an end and Jimmy Carter had become the President, but it was felt that his administration was ineffective. George Bush who had his eyes on the White House had expressed his concerns on the extent of the Federal Loan. Bush had promised that if he was elected President then he would first try to balance the budget.

The Wall Street was being affected by the political situation in the country. By the end of the 70s, the inflation increased drastically; it rose to 13 per cent. The investors were getting desperate and started investing in new avenues like gold, diamonds, real estate, art, other precious metals and packaged commodities and were advising to prepare for the next round of bear phase. Their message was, 'dump shares'.

Their argument against investing in shares was the likelihood of a sharp drop in the earning potential of companies on account of the downturn in the country's economy. In his letter to his shareholders written in 1979, Warren had told that pension fund managers had invested only 9 per cent of the funds in shares. He also said that whichever shares were there in the portfolio of Berkshire, we never felt despondent about the future.

At that time the share prices were down but the fund managers were not buying, they were waiting for the situation to become clear. Manufacturers Hanover Corporation had sold 60 per cent of its investment in shares in the market. A senior Investment Manager Victor Malone had said, "A lot of question remained unanswered."

Janney Montgomery Scott's Vice-Chairman, H.H. Boyle said, "In spite of the sharp drop in share prices, there is no visible enthusiasm to buy shares. People had many doubts in their minds about the future."

This uncertain scenario had been made even more scary by a special report titled, 'End of Shares', published in the August 1979 issue of, 'Business Week'. It seemed as if the article was paying homage to the share market. 'Business Week', had predicted that instead of investing in the share market people will invest in the money market, fast food franchises etc. and pretty soon investing in the share market will become history. The report had said that the shares are available at such cheap prices because no investor was prepared to buy shares. The report had concluded thus, "For good or bad, the American economy must accept the reality of end of equity. Maybe the days of equity may return but it was not going to happen soon."

He was not prepared to accept or digest such wild predictions. The very same week he wrote an article in the 'Forbes' magazine criticizing the Pension Fund Manager's ignorance and feeling of uncertainty:

"Future is never evident. You have to pay a heavy price for any kind of upheaval in the share market. On the other hand, for long-term value-based investors, the uncertainty is like a friend."

Through the article in 'Forbes' magazine he had very clearly expressed his viewpoint on shares. He mentioned that Pension Fund managers were opting for Corporate Bonds where the return was only 1 per cent; they had a simple explanation for it – stocks are not coupon and they are risk prone, particularly considering the state of the market they cannot be relied upon.

Warren believed that this kind of surmise was wrong. Since he could assess the inherent value of a share, he could confidently make such statements– like bonds, shares were also part of corporate assets and shares also could be classified as, 'coupons' because the aspect of corporate earnings was linked to it.

For example, for the companies in the Dow Jones Industrial Index the earning had been 13 per cent of their book value. This statistic can be said to be impressive. Whereas, those index shares were now available below their book value. When Warren visualised with his eyes closed, then the stocks in the Dow Index seemed like, 'Dow Bond' with a return of 13 per cent, which was many times of the returns through bonds. For a patient investor the returns could be much higher.

In spite of the bear market, his company's shares were rising. Berkshire's shares were quoting at 290 dollars per share and Warren's wealth had grown to 149 million dollars. But the interesting thing was that Warren, whose salary was only 50,000 dollars, was not prepared to sell his shares. Nor did he allow distribution of dividend, which would have reduced the capital of the company. It may have created some hindrance in his working for which he was not at all prepared.

Warren was feeling the pressure on account of bearing the expenses of two families so he told Omaha's Charlie Header, "Whatever I had received I have invested in Berkshire. So I will have to arrange some money from outside."

Towards the end of the 70s, Warren had purchased some shares in his account. He was prepared to take risk with his own money. He invested in the shares of Teledyne even though he was in a dilemma. The dilemma was that either he would lose the entire money or he would make a killing.

"It is amazing to note how easily he managed it!" An employee of Berkshire told," He had thoroughly investigated the company. In no time he made a lot of money."

When a friend suggested that he should try his luck in the real estate market, then Warren replied, "When it is easy for me to earn money in the stock market, why should I invest in the real estate market." According to Broker Earl Ravel, Warren had made 3 million dollars in no time."

In spite of becoming extremely wealthy, Warren had a simple lifestyle. He used to drive his Lincoln car himself and reach his office, where his 5 employees used to manage the corporate affairs of Berkshire Hathaway. In his free time, he liked to play bridge, read books on business, watch games and talk shows. He used to take Astrid to, 'Garrett's restaurant for eating outside. The owner of this restaurant was his old classmate.

With time Warren's circle– his friends, his companies, his articles, were spreading outside Omaha. His 40th birthday celebrations were arranged in one of the Golf Courses in Omaha. In 1980, on his 50th birthday, Susie had arranged a grand party in New York's Metropolitan Club. The party was attended by Warren's several classmates, friends and other respected people. On this occasion Susie had sung a song and dedicated to Warren.

None of the guests in the party could visualize Warren as a businessman. The way Warren was attired, his mannerism his expressions, nobody/none of the guests could visualize Warren as a businessman. He looked like a professor. Nobody could guess from his gestures that the per share price of his holding company Berkshire Hathaway had become 875 dollars.

Next year, Warren barely survived an accident. Warren and Charlie Munger's Money Manager Rick Green's wife suddenly expired. Warren went from Omaha to California to meet Green.

"I am feeling extremely distressed." Green said.

Warren replied, "I can understand the agony which you must be going through. When my father had died, I had also faced it." After being quiet for a little while he said, "You and your son take a flight and come to Minnesota Island, where Charlie Munger stays, we will spend 3-4 days together.

As per their scheduled program, they reached Charlie Munger's cabin by the side of a lake on Minnesota Island. Charlie took them for fishing in a motorboat. Seeing the extreme speed at which Charlie was driving, Green requested him to reduce the speed. Munger being short sighted suddenly applied full brakes, as a result of which the motorboat dived into the lake. Warren started drowning. Green somehow pulled him out of the water. Later they took the incident lightly, but Warren was shaken by the feeling of drowning.

Green was duly impressed by Warren's sympathetic behaviour, who had postponed all his activities to boost his morale.

Green said "He has a magnanimous heart. But people do not notice this aspect. For me, his sympathy is like a gift to me."

The popularity of Warren's letters kept on rising on Wall Street. Bankers were distributing copies of his reports. For the first time, Warren found that people were emulating him. People, who were eager to read the letters written by him, also bought the shares of Berkshire Hathaway.

Charlie Munger said that it was providence that Warren was managing a public limited company. If he wanted, he could have easily set up and managed his own company. But then it might not have been possible for him to play the role of an expert adviser. He could express himself freely through his letters. He used to pick any aspect of the operations of Berkshire and present his viewpoint, commentary on it. Even when talking about any problems related to accounts or any matters related to insurance, he used to explain the complex issues in easy to understand words. For the business world his letters were thus extraordinary. Any person who would peruse say, General Motors report would do so to find out details about its working. He was not at all curious to know about the report writer or company's officials. On the other hand, Warren used to discuss issues like human weaknesses, greed, suspicions etc. He used to discuss the issues freely. He usually presented the complex principles of investing in an interesting manner, in layman's language. He could not only teach the principles of business to the owner of, 'Washington Post', Katherine Graham but he possessed capability to teach them to Wall Street and the whole of America.

When Jack Barney, who knew Warren, used to read his reports, it seemed like adrenalin was flowing throughout his body. A 19 year old young businessman from Trinidad was overwhelmed after reading Warren's report. He said that, "God has sent a priceless gift to me; it is a copy of the annual report of Berkshire Hathaway".

The simple reason for this was that in the journey of American capitalism, no other company could match Berkshire Hathaway's success. Several capitalists and intellectuals have been born in America, one greater than the other but Warren's personality was most remarkable and singular. Warren would add humour in his articles to make them interesting and had assumed the role of a lecturer. Warren was gaining popularity because he used to explain the complex subject of investing in a simple language which even a person with average intelligence, could easily understand.

In the 80s, Warren had discussed the dangers of inflation in the annual report. He wrote – "Care must be taken to keep the prices stable, like it is required to preserve virginity; as it cannot be regained once it is lost." He had also expressed the possibility of the demise of long-term bonds on account of rising inflation. But his prediction did not materialize.

Yet Warren's foresight had alerted him and his shareholders to meet the challenges that could arise on account of inflation. His prediction on the effects of inflation on the insurance business turned out to be true. On account of the rising inflation the bond prices were falling and most of the investments of the insurance companies was in bonds. Warren could understand that the insurance business was going to suffer losses. After the drop in bond prices, the insurance companies were in a quandary to sell their assets to pay the claims. Such companies were losing their capital. Warren also believed that the money which the insurance companies had invested in bonds was not their money, but that of the policyholders. The policyholders had the right over this money.

The insurance companies could have cancelled some policies to save themselves from paying the claims. Berkshire had invested minimal amounts in long-term bonds, about which Warren had said that it was like blocking your capital at fixed rates for 30 years. In the current inflation scenario, it would have been suicidal to fix the prices of Berkshires threads for 2010 in advance.

In fact, it is not possible to save yourself by just becoming aware of the dangers of inflation. Warren told that when he had acquired control of Berkshire then one could buy half an ounce of gold with the price of its one share. In 15 years Berkshire's per share price had risen to

335.85 dollars from 19.46 dollars and yet one could only buy half an ounce of gold in that price.

At this time the only option which he had, to invest in such companies, which could face the challenges posed by inflation. He said that companies like Post Cereal and Winston Cigarettes will be able to increase their incomes at the rate the inflation rises. He invested in companies like Aluminum Company of America, Cleveland-Cliffs Iron Company, Handy and Harman, Kaiser Aluminum and Chemicals etc. However, Warren kept on reminding his shareholders that neither he nor Berkshire had any firm solution to meet the crisis.

According to Warren inflation was like a, 'Giant corporate woodworm', which everyday gobbled up humongous amounts of invested dollars and did not at all bother about the health of its digestive system.

On Wall Street, on account of inflation corporate assets were being liquidated. Companies like people were despondent and were not prepared to convert their cash holding into any other form. In the beginning of the 80s, the activity of taking over of companies intensified. Big companies like Del Monte, National Airlines, Seven Up, Studebaker and Tropicana etc. were taken over. Seeing all this, Warren became a critic of Wall Street.

Warren believed that Corporate CEOs were entering into irrational deals. According to Darwin, the breed of CEOs were very energetic and they were assessing their capabilities based on their positions. They were not taking decisions according to Warren's profit-based principle, which Warren considered as the sole logical objective. Unlike Warren, who used to buy smaller companies at discounted prices, these CEOs liked to buy big companies at premium prices. They were so much self-centered and egoistic that even after paying such exorbitant prices, they hoped to make profit. Warren wrote–

"Several of these CEOs had heard the story of the prince who was caged as a parrot and when the princess kissed it, it again turned into a prince. In the same manner, these CEOs hoped that companies will start generating profits by their magical kiss. We have seen many such kisses, but never seen the miracle.

Warren had expressed this view in the annual report of 1981, when the wave of mergers had just started. Next year he had expressed his views on the changed circumstances. Many CEOs were issuing new shares to pay for the assets that were taken over. Warren drew attention to the negative effects of this new wave, which on the surface appeared to be a normal phenomenon. He argued that the acquirers were not only buying, but were also selling. With every new share issued, the shareholding of the existing shareholders was diminishing. The CEOs were trying to cover up this fact by presenting it as something which was dear to their hearts, "Your company is acquiring another company." Whereas, the true picture would have been clear only if the truth had been revealed. It was only by selling a part of their company that the said company was being acquired.

Why was recourse being taken to lying? Most of the shares including the acquired shares were available at low prices. Then why were the CEO's of the acquiring companies getting into unfavourable deals.

Warren suggested that such Managers and Directors needed to sharpen their thought process. They needed to introspect on the manner in which they were selling part of their shares, were they also prepared to sell the entire company? If no, then why were they selling part share in the company at throwaway prices?

Warren wrote that, "The sum total of all the little bits of managerial follies will only lead to a huge folly, not any miracle."

Warren was disturbed by the CEOs expanding their own domains by frittering away the shareholders money, whereas it was their duty to take care of the shareholders interests. Warren thought that such Managers should have made their career in government jobs.

Warren was mocking the corporate abbots by comparing them to bureaucrats. Even though in his personal life, Warren had cordial relations with several CEOs. He used to attend their meetings also. In his articles, he used to refrain from naming anyone. He preferred to maintain his distance from his corporate associates. He always considered the wrong doers as white collared criminals. He wrote, "It is safer to loot huge sums of money with the power of the pen as compared to looting even small sums by pointing a gun."

Warren believed that since they were dealing with public money, the Managers bear a major responsibility. He gave examples of how in his life, he fulfilled this responsibility. In 1980, consequent to the change in Federal Laws, Berkshire had to grant the status of an independent company to Rockford Bancorp. Warren estimated that the valuation of the Bank was 4 per cent of Berkshire's total valuation. He then gave the option to the shareholders to hold the shares of Berkshire and Bank as per their choice. Warren did not keep any option for himself. He was going to hold the remaining shares. His principle was that the person who cuts the cake must be satisfied with leftover piece.

With a similar approach in 1981, Warren presented a Model Corporate Charity Plan. The plan was designed by Charlie Munger. Under this plan, for a million shares (at that time the share price was 470 dollars), the company would donate a sum of 2 dollars per share to the charity specified by the shareholders. That is, if a shareholder had 100 shares, then he could ask the company to donate 200 dollars to his choice charity. In other public limited companies, the decisions-related to charities were taken by the CEO and Directors, the money was taken from the shareholders also. Warren considered this as having double standards. He wrote, "Several corporate managers criticized the government for spending the taxpayer's money, on their whims; but why don't they introspect themselves for using the shareholders' money on their whims."

By such statements and actions, Warren was projecting Berkshire as a company with a unique image. He was shaping this partnership company on the lines of a public limited company. There were several of his former partners, amongst the thousands of shareholders. The purpose of his letters to the shareholders was to make them feel as if were his partners and a group could be formed. Thus, they remained associated with him.

It cannot be denied that Warren's ways were unique. Most of the CEOs did not care about their shareholders. For them the investors were faceless and changing entities. They never felt the necessity to associate with them. On the other hand, Warren believed in having a permanent association with his shareholders. In his letter to them he had compared his company to a café, where the customer liked to eat and likes to come back repeatedly.

While holidaying on Laguna Beach with his family, Warren used to write the 7800 worded letter to the shareholders on a yellow legal pad. His sister Roberta was living abroad for the last one year, while writing the letter he used to perceive that he was writing the letter to update her on his business. Carol Loomis, who used work for the 'Fortune', magazine edit his letter; but Warren's particular style, as if he was conversing with someone, was retained. His letter had a touch of humour and even serious matters were presented in an interesting manner.

Warren had gained expertise in writing annual reports as he had been ceaselessly studying annual reports. The other company's reports were more like publicity documents in which the management's capabilities were highlighted to allure the investors. They contained a brief and formal message from the CEO. Mostly these reports were written by someone else on behalf of the CEO. In these reports, the thing which most irked Warren, was the fact that the CEOs shirked from personally addressing the shareholders.

Warren used to be critical of CEOs, who kept changing their goals; and when they got disappointing results, they started seeking for lame excuses.

In Berkshire's annual report, the company's internal state was described so realistically, that the investor was able to easily understand the true picture. To achieve this, Warren used simple vocabulary. In the early days, the type of analysis which Warren used to present to his partners on the likely profit, similarly considering the shareholders of Berkshire to be his partners, he would intimately share what was in his heart. He used to honestly accept his short-comings and describe them without suppressing any aspect.

□

12

Warren and Madam B

Warren used to frequently think that if instead of a public limited company, he had had to invest in his own enterprise and manage it, what kind of experience it might have been for him.

With such thoughts crossing his mind, in summer of 1983, he entered Nebraska Furniture Mart, a store built on a 43 acre plot in Omaha. The owner of this Mart was a 4 feet 10 inches tall woman named Rose Blumkin. She was addressed as 'Madam B', by the people of Omaha. At the age of 90, she used to work 12 hours every day. For Warren she was like an idol, who had set up a massive furniture empire with an initial investment of 500 dollars only.

Warren asked, 'Madam B', are you prepared to sell your business to Berkshire Hathaway?

Madam B said, "Yes."

Warren asked, "For how much."

Madam B replied, "60 million dollars."

Both shook hands and Warren took her signatures on a single page agreement. Warren had succeeded in making his life's biggest deal. After a few days Warren paid a cheque for 90 per cent of the deal amount to Madam B, 10 per cent was owned by the Blumkin family. 'Madam B' did not even look at the cheque, folded it and kept it and said, "Mister Buffett, we can drive our competitor's out of business."

The firmness, determination and understanding which was there in Madam B's personality, reminded Warren of his businessman grandfather's personality. Warren was tremendously impressed by Madam B's success story and it used to inspire him.

She was born as Rose Corlic in 1893 in a small village called Belarus near Minsk in Russia during the Czar era. She used to sleep on the floor with her seven brothers and sisters. Her father was unemployed and her mother used to feed the family by managing a small grocery store. Seeing the hardship which her mother was facing, Rose started helping her in the store from the age of six.

There was no money for the children to attend school. Rose never attended school. She sought help from a rich family and learned to read and write a bit. She had learnt to toil and become independent from her mother. At the age of 13, she started working in a store selling dry goods in Minsk. At the age of 16, she started managing that store and supervising five male employees.

In 1914, Rose was married to Issadot Blumkin, who moved to America. Rose was to follow him later, but before she could proceed to America, war started. In the winter of 1917, when Europe was in shambles and anarchy was wide-spread in Russia, she boarded the trans-Siberian train. She was stopped by a Russian soldier; she did not have a passport. Rose told the soldier that she was going to buy leather for the army and she will get a bottle of vodka for him when she returns. She reached Japan *via* Manchester. From there she boarded a boat and reached America after 6 weeks. In 1919, she settled in Omaha with her husband. Even though she was in dire straits, she called her parents and siblings to Omaha. Rose's husband was running a, 'used clothes' shop. To help her family, Rose started selling furniture from the basement of her house. She did not know English, but her children who were studying in English medium school, taught her English.

In 1937, with her savings of 500 dollars, Rose rented a shop on Farnam Street. After a lot of deliberation, she named the store, 'Nebraska Furniture Mart.' Her business philosophy was, 'Sell cheap and tell the truth.' The big companies manufacturing furniture thought that by selling the furniture at cheaper prices, she could spoil the image of their brand, so they refused to supply to her. But she did not give up. She would travel to Chicago or Kansas by train and buy furniture from the retailers. When the shops stock was sold out, she moved the stock kept in the house to the shop. Rose approached the bank for loan but her application was rejected. The experience left her with feeling of revulsion toward banks. With an iron will, she would continue to work non-stop for the whole week, without any break. She liked to sell the furniture to the middle-income customers, who believed in paying on time.

In 1944, Mohawk Corporate Mill filed a case against her. They charged that she was violating the product pricing law. The carpet which Mohawk Mill was selling at the rate of 7.25 dollars per yard, Rose was selling the same carpet at the rate of 4.95 dollars per yard. The Judge dismissed the case stating that it was frivolous. Next day the Judge bought carpets worth 1400 dollars from Nebraska Furniture Mart.

Rose dealt firmly with her employees and her family members. Her behaviour was affectionate only towards her well mannered son Luis. On several occasions, Luis reinstated employees by sweetly counseling them after reprimanded and dismissed by Rose. Luis was adept at quelling Rose's anger.

Rose or, 'Madam B's' success formula was simple– she would buy furniture in bulk, control her expenses and pay special attention on saving. Normally, she would sell on 10 per cent profit margin; but occasionally allowed special discount to her customers. If a newly wed couple came to buy furniture, then 'Madam B' allowed a higher discount, because she knew that the couple could come again to make more purchases.

For the people of Omaha, the Mart had become an integral part of their lives. It was unlikely that there was any family in Omaha, who did not have furniture bought from the Mart. Ageing had not diminished 'Madam B's' enthusiasm or working-capabilities. Once storm demolished the roof of her store but she continued selling the furniture. On another occasion, the store caught fire. 'Madam B' gifted a TV set to the fire brigade employees. She was never on holiday. She used to say, "I do not lie. I do not deceive anyone. I do not promise anything which I cannot fulfil. Sticking to these principles has helped me to attain success."

After buying the store, Warren did not want to manage it himself. He wanted a manager, who would manage the store according to his style of functioning. Warren felt that he could not get a Manager, better than 'Madam B.' He appointed, 'Madam B' as the store's Manager on an annual salary of 300,000 dollars per annum. He always used to refer 'Madam B', as one of his great idols.

□

13

Most Prosperous Period of His Life

After Susie's death when her Will was read, everyone was surprised, even though most of the clauses were not unexpected. Susie had willed most of the shares of Berkshire, valued at approximately 3 billion dollars to Susan Thompson Buffett Foundation. This Foundation was now being managed by her daughter. She left approximately 50 million dollars to her children's charity, while each of her children received 10 million dollars and each grandchild received 100,000 dollars.

She was generous towards people whom she liked, even though it was not evident on account of her husband's influence. She also left a number of friends and employee's substantial sums including $8 million to John McCabe and $1 million to Ron Parks. The names of Cathleen Cole and her husband's names were also included. Before her death, she had made changes in her Will through a new lawyer. The changes made by her in the Will had surprised everyone.

Susie had never accepted the split in her life and had left this aspect undefined till the end of her life. She used to live for others but this reality was not expressed in words till her end.

Warren considered his wife as his idol and was in love with her for a very long time. She kept him in touch with the outside world and kept the family bonded. After her death, whenever Warren looked at her photo, tears would roll down his eyes. In spite of this, he did not break down; nor did he isolate himself or think of committing suicide out of despondence. Though, Susie had earlier expressed the possibility of occurrence of such actions. However, Warren continued to grieve and for next two months; he appeared extremely weary. After that, as it happens with most of the people, he gradually fell into his normal routine. With loving memory of his departed wife in his heart, he started his life anew.

His elder son said, "His relationship with mother was sincere and there can be no doubt about it. He depended a lot on mother. But my father is a fighter. People, who had thought that he would be shattered by mother's death, apparently did not know him very well. My Daddy's will can never break down, he is inherently strong, even though it may not be evident on the surface. The heights which he has attained are due to his strong determination."

Warren was able to recover on account of his mental perseverance and was successful in overcoming the fixation that, "Susie will take care of everything." He was ready to face the ground realities. As time passed, he began accepting the reality of Susie's death and started bonding with his children on new grounds.

According to his sister Berta, "At the time of her death, Susie had handed over her inheritance of strength, emotional attachment and generosity to Warren. Unexpected changes had started occurring in Warren's personal life. He had started tackling those emotional issues which he had left for his wife to tackle. He had become sensitive towards his children's feelings and had started taking care of them.

His daughter, Susie Jr. had promptly assumed the responsibility of her mother's legacy and taken over its leadership. She liked philanthropic activities and for past several years had been preparing for such work. She engaged herself in expanding the philanthropic activities. She did not consider managing two foundations a burden, but considered it as a challenging opportunity.

His musician son, Peter was presenting his musical production 'spirit the seventh fire', in Washington's National Mall. The program had been organized during a function of 'National Museum of American Indian.' Over phone he told his father, "Dad our presentation is going to be an amazing feat." After telling this to his father, he realized that had his mother been alive, he would have told it to his mother, who would have informed his father. He felt happy that he had communicated with his father directly. Warren grouped his friends and they departed for Washington to see the program. Before the presentation of 'Spirit', Peter had released 13 Albums. While enjoying the program, Warren felt a distinct attachment towards his son. This feeling was arising not only because of Peter's success but also on account of the fact that they were making efforts to share their lives.

When 'Spirit' was presented in Philadelphia, it was declared as a historic presentation.

Warren's elder son, Howard had published two books on photography, 'On the Edge' and 'Tapestry of Life'. He had also organized several exhibitions. His foundation office still appeared like a teenager's bedroom, a museum filled with odd things. But his business sense had improved. He was a member on the Boards of Lindsay Manufacturing and Connemara. He had dismissed two CEOs. He believed in saving and he had invested in Berkshire. Howard was emotionally attached to his mother and used to yearn for his father's shield over him from the very beginning. Now he had got an opportunity to establish a distinct relationship with his father. He, along with Devon bought a house in Omaha so that he could stay close to his father.

The events after Susie's death had deeply affected Astrid. She had lost a close well-wisher. She then realized that Susie's life was running on parallel tracks in which a particular type of life had been out of sight. After maintaining a cordial relations with Susie for many years and tied to an unconventional marriage, was living like a role model, suddenly felt that everything was collapsing. She knew the manner in which Warren had been emotionally tied to Susie and this was disconcerting her. However, gradually Warren was also realizing that by following Susie's arrangement Astrid had paid a heavy price and for the past several years both of them had been overlooking it. He blamed himself for it and began improving the relationship anew. After recovering from his grief Warren started making Astrid a part of his public life.

In the month of December Warren used to gift cheques of substantial amounts to his grandchildren for Christmas. He also used to bear their education expenses but he did not like to pay for any wasteful expenses. He always counselled everyone through a covering letter on how they should spend the money. He would write, "Use some of it on entertainment, pay off your debts but I would not like you to spend it on unnecessary things. You will get your next cheque next year."

Warren did not send the gift cheques for Peter's adopted daughters– Nicole and Erica. But Susie used to like Nicole and Erica. Both of them had attended Susie's cremation. Susie had left a sum of $100,000 for each of them in her Will. But just 10 days after the cremation Warren told Peter, "I do not consider them as my grandchildren. I am not going to leave anything for them in my Will."

Peter could not believe it. He asked him," Are you really going to do so?"

Warren was undeterred on his word. Since Susie's Will had conferred the status of grandchildren to those girls. It seemed that Warren had developed a sense of attachment towards money. Peter was under the impression that if his Dad excluded the girl's from his Will or did not send the Christmas cheque, the girls will not come to know of the reason.

Warren and Astrid celebrated the New Year's Eve with Sharon Osberg and her husband David Smith at Warren's house in Marine County in California. He was playing bridge with Sharon, David and Gates, while Astrid was busy in shopping. In the beginning of November, Warren's fears that Berkshire's Board would be suppressed under Gates imposing personality were allayed. He had invited Gates to join the Board of Berkshire.

Sharon and Gates were discussing the challenges which the Buffett Foundation was likely to face. The possibility of a dramatic change seemed likely after one year of Warren's death on donating billions of dollars. There was no history of any Foundation having succeeded in bringing about such a change because no other foundation had tried it. Gates Foundation was an exception; otherwise no other Foundation had received such a massive donation.

Warren had also been pondering over this issue. In winter, he had arranged for a video recording of a question-answer session with the Foundation's Trustees. He wanted to ensure that the Trustees clearly understood his wishes. He wanted to eliminate the possibility of any fraudulent action after his death as it had happened in the case of Walter Annenberg.

In the beginning of 2005, Sharon had met Warren in Omaha and after praising Gates had asked if he would consider making a donation to the Gates Foundation after his death. Warren did not promise her anything at that time, even though before Susie's death, he had thought about donating some amount to the Gates Foundation.

Charlie Munger was also in agreement with this thought. He believed that like Warren, Gates also believed in staying away from the beaten path. He was only 50 years old and he would utilise the money properly.

Warren's long standing belief was that he could best serve the society by continuing to maintain the pace of his earnings and there was no need to distribute it. He had planned to return the money to the society after his death; but he was also apprehensive that if he died before finalizing the donation, it may not be utilized properly. He had been changing gradually over the years. From a child who had stolen his sister's bicycle and selling barbells; a father who refused his children's request for money; a person who gifted thousands of dollars to his children on their birthday after every five years; a father who had bought a heart shaped pink diamond ring for his daughter. In spite of all these things, he had definite ideas about money but after Susie's death he started re-evaluating the ideas. He had made up his mind to take specific action now itself to resolve the apprehensions of the future. It did not mean that it was easy for him to overtake time.

It was his birthday, nearly a year after Susie's death. He could not believe that he had been through 75 springs. He started thinking about people with long lives and good health. His mother had lived for 92 years; his aunt Cary had lived for 97 years, 90 year old Walter Schloss was still playing tennis and his idol Rose Blumkin was still enjoying life.

His 75th birthday was celebrated at Sharon and David's house. In the party Astrid, Bill Gates and his sister Berta were also there. The birthday cake was prepared with white chocolate and it was shaped like a 100 dollar bill. David had invited an American girl of Chinese origin on Saturday morning to play ping-pong with Warren.

Sharon had invited an artist who was going to teach the basics of drawing to Warren and Gates. The drawing which Warren had made depicted trees-shaped liked lollipops. The ping-pong competition was declared as the most exciting event. It was decided that the ping-pong competition video be shown in the next share-holders meeting.

Before 2003, Warren's desire to publicise himself was fulfilled through interviews and shareholders' meetings. Warren was cautious while dealing with the media. He used to adopt a diplomatic attitude. But when Susie fell sick, for whatever reason, he tried to draw their attention. His attachment towards TV cameras heightened. It became difficult for him to stay away from publicity for long. He assisted in the making of several documentaries. He would extend interviews with Charlie Roe for hours. He was appearing on CNBC regularly.

On one hand, he appeared to be obsessed with the media, on the other hand, his mind was completely focused on Berkshire. He was capable of rapidly switching his roles. After the induction of Bill Gates in the Berkshire's Board, he had introduced a monitoring system in his organization– the system allowed any employee to report any kind of short-coming. He also wanted to ensure that Board of Berkshire became self-reliant in taking decisions even in his absence. To achieve this end, he organized several board meetings in which he did not participate. Even today, he participates in the investment activities of the company with the same concentration and devotion as he used to do in his youth.

After the 9/11 incident, the Federal Reserve had dramatically cut the interest rates and the share market had started showing signs of weakening. In his letter to the share-holders, written in 2004, Warren had stated "I had expected new investment of several billion dollars, which would have created new avenues of earning. But I am surprised, I see only very few attractive securities which can be bought. Next year Berkshire made four small investments and one large investment. The large investment was in the renewable energy sector. The company's name was Mid American Energy. The oil prices were continuously rising so the importance of renewable energy was growing. This company's CEO, David Sokol was being rumoured to become Warren's successor, even though Warren never said anything about it.

Warren had in his report expressed his doubts on the strengthening of the dollar and believed it was going to weaken. After his first report, dollar kept on becoming stronger and his views were criticized in the financial papers-magazines. He reduced his hedged positions to buy foreign stocks but maintained his stance. On derivatives he wrote–

"Long time back Mark Twain had said that if somebody wants to catch his cat's tail, then he cannot experience the feeling without actually doing so. I discuss derivatives every year for two reasons. The first one is personal and disturbing. At the time of buying Gen Ray, Charlie and I knew that it will create problems and we had told its management that we wanted to exit from this business. It was my responsibility to ensure it. Instead of tackling the issue, I wasted several years in trying to avoid the operation. It was a futile effort. Because we could not find a fitting solution for the crisis, which had been in existence for decades, it was not easy for me to exit the business." Warren was referring to the period when he had appointed a new Director and allowed him sometime to expand the business. But later this turned out to be a loss-making proposition.

He wrote– "Whenever problem arises, may be in personal life or in business, it must be tackled immediately."

"The other reason for referring to these problems regularly is that our experiences can help the Directors, Auditors and Regulators."

Warren suspected that like the decade of the 70s, the investment sentiment was not likely to improve soon. In spite of this, he kept his search open and continued evaluating new ideas.

In 2004, he borrowed a voluminous book from his broker which appeared like a compilation of several telephone directories. The book contained a detailed record of South Korea's stock market. He had been tracking the world economy. He was on the lookout for a country and market, which had not drawn much attention and was relatively cheap. South Korea's stock market fitted the bill. He spent a lot of nights and studied the book in-depth. He was finding it difficult to understand the numbers and other details. He felt that it was necessary for him to learn a new business language through which he could properly understand a different business culture. So he got another book and tried to understand the important details of Korean accounting. It thus became simpler for him to understand the riddle of numbers.

When he fully understood their shares listing procedure, he started comparing the accounting details of their companies and selecting them. While doing this he recalled the days he had spent under Graham-Neumann, when he used to sit near the ticket machine wearing a grey jacket. From the hundreds of pages accounts of different companies he was trying to identify the important numbers and checking for their sequential consistency. He was successful in selecting the cream shares from the thousands of Korean shares. He was regularly noting all his comments on a yellow pad and was able to prepare a brief list.

The list was so brief that he was able to record it on a single sheet. He discussed the list with a visitor. It contained the names of about a dozen companies. A few of them were well-known companies but mostly they were smaller companies.

Warren said, "Please see how I have prepared it. These companies believe in winning. If you check for these companies on the Korean Stock Exchange site, on the net, you will find that instead of ticket symbols they use numbers. In case it is not a blue chip share, then they place a zero at the end of the number. You can see such statistics every night. I can name five brokerages who are big buyers and five brokerages who are big sellers. You will have to open a special account in a Korean bank and it is not easy to do so. I am trying to learn the procedure. For me it is like picking up friendship with a new girl. These are good companies and their shares are still cheap. They are only priced equal to their next 5 years earnings, whereas their business can be relied upon. Though half the companies names sound like porn films. These companies produce basic things like steel, cement, flour and electricity. People will continue to buy these things for the next 10 years. These companies have a good presence in the Korean market, which is unlikely to change. Some of these companies are also exporting to China and Japan. Due to certain factors these companies have till now not come in the limelight. I am not an expert on foreign currency, but I think that buying these shares will be a profitable investment."

"The main reason why these share are cheap, is North Korea. In case North Korea attacks South Korea, the whole world can be affected. China, Japan and the other Asian countries can be involved in the conflict. The outcome of the war cannot even be imagined. North Korea seems to have developed capabilities to produce nuclear weapons. I think that it is the most dangerous country in the world. In spite of this I am prepared to take the risk, because I know that China and Japan will be able to stop the devastation of war."

"When you invest in shares, then there is always a risk. The future is uncertain forever. I think that for the next few years these share will continue to perform and I am prepared to hold them for that duration."

Warren had found a new game to play and a new puzzle to solve. He immersed himself in the search of new investment opportunities with the enthusiasm of his younger days.

During his visit to Harvard Business School for a lecture, he was asked how Buffett Foundation, which was the world's richest organization could benefit the society. He replied "I, am not doing any good to the society by multiplying my wealth so I am thinking of donating my wealth for the benefit of the society."

Nobody said anything. Though nobody realized that through his reply had clearly hinted of making a directional change in his life.

After his lecture, he had talked about Gates Foundation. He had praised the welfare work being done by Bill and Melinda Gates. He had said that Gates Foundation was working wisely and its principles were being followed in the best manner. He said that he liked their style of giving charity without any publicity. They never wanted their names or the foundations name to appear anywhere.

A clear plan had started evolving in his mind in the beginning of 2006. He was satisfied with his children's work, who were managing their own Foundations. But now he could not even find any sense of security which he felt in the presence of his wife Susie. Emotional power worked at a level higher than consciousness. When he had given Susie the liberty spending money for charitable activities, he had not assessed her ability to serve mankind. After living together for decades with Susie, they had developed a relationship of trust which had generated his faith in his wife's wisdom and ability to take decisions. Everything had changed after her death. He told about his change of heart to Tom Murphy, during his daughter's marriage. He also told about the change in him to Sharon Osberg. He wanted to donate his wealth at the earliest. But this decision was still a thought; he did not have a plan.

It took several months to prepare a plan because it was vast and complex.

He started telling about his plan to people, who might be affected by it. His sisters were pleased by his plan. Bertie told him that it was his best decision. Doris, who was managing Sunshine Lady Foundation, also said that it was a superb decision, because she knew that it was a very difficult task to donate billions of dollars wisely.

On 26th of June, 2006 Warren announced that he will donate 83 per cent of his share in Berkshire Hathaway, which was valued at 37 billion dollars at that time to a group of foundations within a few years time. In the history of service towards mankind, such a massive sum had never been donated earlier. The biggest charity in the world, 'Bill and Melinda Gates Foundation', was to receive 5 shares out of every 6 shares, which he personally owned. This was going to unite two great personalities and benefit the entire world. Warren desired that his donation be used in welfare activities according to his wishes but at the same time the foundations had freedom to decide on the amount they wished to spend on those activities. Fully understanding the impact of his decision, he allocated the balance shares valued at 6 billion dollars to his children's and his wife's foundations. His three children's foundations were allocated 1 billion dollars each and Susan Thompson Buffett Foundation was allocated 3 billion dollars. His children never imagined that their personal foundations could get such huge sums and that too while Warren was still alive. In the first annual instalment, Gates

Foundation received shares worth 1.5 billion dollars, his children's foundations received shares worth 50 million dollars each and Susan Thompson Buffett Foundation received shares worth 150 million dollars. There could be variations in the amounts deemed to be paid, based on the price of the Berkshires shares prevailing at that time, in all probability amounts would continue to rise. The second richest man in the world was donating his entire wealth, and he was doing it without registering his name anywhere. He continued to earn money throughout his life but he did not set up any foundation in his name i.e. Warren Buffett Foundation nor did he open any hospital, college or University in his name; did not get his name inscribed on any structure. While donating, he was not bothered about highlighting his name or controlling the donated amount. He was donating to a foundation that he had selected after considering its expertise and merit. He had not set up another empire to donate and thus shown a new way to donate; very different from the customary convention. Till today not a single big donor had taken such a step.

Rockefeller Mankind Service Organisation's advisor Doug Bower said, "It was a momentous moment in the field of service to mankind. A new milestone has been laid."

Even though Warren's action was surprising but considering his attitude possibly it could be considered normal. A person who was an unconventional thinker and crisis handler wanted to stay away from vain display and wasteful expenditure. Gates Foundation had received the funds but they had to use the first instalment quickly. This decision was uncharacteristic, highly personal, an extraordinary example and as expected attracted attention. But on the other hand, it could be considered as an unerring decision taken by Warren in his own exceptional style.

He had astounded the entire world by donating most of his wealth; but his donation *modus operandi* was such that he retained the funds till the time he physically transferred the shares. At the same time in a single move, he had announced donation of most of his life's earning and had initiated the process of distributing millions of dollars. A boy who would not allow even his family members to touch his piggy bank, in which he deposit his coins had today become the world's greatest donor, who was donating billions of dollars for philanthropy.

While announcing his decision to donate Warren had said in his speech, "Fifty years back I had a meeting with seven people. We had formed a small partnership company with an initial sum of 150,000 dollars. They had thought that I would be able to manage their money better they could do so themselves.

"Fifty years after that event, on a particular day it occurred to me that I was myself the best person to give away the money appropriately. This argument is entirely logical. Often people do not get the opportunity to think. They are often heard wondering– who will be able to take care of my money? Such people usually give the responsibility of taking care of their money to the people whom they consider capable. But they overlook the persons who are active in the field of philanthropy. They handover the responsibility one of their trusted friend or colleague to take care of their money but they are no longer there to see how it is being utilized.

"So I consider myself fortunate as the job of serving the mankind is more difficult than doing business. One has to find solution for vital issues, which have been solved in the past by applying wisdom and with aid of money. So it is more important to search talent in field of philanthropy as compared to searching talent in the investment field.

"I have been lucky. I was born in America in 1930 and have been lucky from my birth. I got wonderful parents, good education and I was brought up in such a manner which enabled me to succeed in deriving benefit from the society. Had I been born earlier or in some other country, it's possible that I might not have been so lucky. In a market-based economy it is essential to learn the art of wealth allocation and this ability can yield desired results.

"I always thought that wealth is something which must be returned to the society. I don't believe in dynastic wealth, particularly when we see the 6 billion people, who face hardships. We get opportunities to serve the people with our wealth. My wife also supported this thinking.

"It was obvious that Bill Gates had a brilliant mind and his target was correct. He was wholeheartedly serving the mankind, rising above sex, religion, colour or geographical boundaries. So when I was faced with the question– to whom should I donate? It became easier to decide."

Warren was impressed by the Gates Foundations Mission statement which stated, 'Every life is equally precious.' The foundation's objective was to eliminate the inequality in the world and improve the life of mankind. The organization was focusing on providing health care and education. The Gates couple considered themselves as organisers, who were trying to find permanent solution to the countless difficulties being faced by mankind in consultation with persons with brilliant minds.

Even though after Susie's death, Warren's thinking had undergone many changes but in certain matters his beliefs remained unchanged. Allen Green Berg, who was managing the Susan Thompson Warren Foundation learned that foundation was only going to get 6 million dollars and not 45 billion dollars. He was expecting the larger amount. Warren sent him a message through Susie Jr. that he should prepare the future plans after proper consideration and he should not consider himself any slighter because of the smaller amount. Susie Jr. was Allen's new Boss and his former wife. Allen realized that even with 6 million dollars, his foundation will be considered as one of the top 10 richest foundations in the world and he heaved a sigh of relief.

All the people associated with the donation were satisfied. Even though Warren had announced the donation, its disbursement was spread over many years.

Warren's donation announcement had a deep impact elsewhere also. Hong Kong's Cinema Star Jackie Chan announced that he would donate half of his wealth. Asia's richest man Li Ka-Sing announced donation of one third of his total wealth of 19 billion dollars to his charitable foundation. Mexico's richest man Carlos Slim initially made mockery of Warren and Gates philanthropy, but after a few months changed his mind and announced that he would also donate his wealth. Gates set up a new department in his foundation which communicated and followed up with persons who were desirous of donating. A 7 year old girl donated her entire savings of 35 dollars to Gates Foundation.

Gates Foundation's influence was spreading all over the world and funds were pouring in. The objectives of this foundation were similar to Warren's objectives. According to which, carefully selected serious hardships were being funded to solve them. This foundation was distinct from the other foundations in the world. In most of headquarters of foundation, money was wasted. The workers were whimsical and the philanthropic activities were neglected. By the end of 2006, foundations like the Rockefeller Foundation, impressed by the working of the Gates Foundation brought about changes in their working styles.

After Warren's announcement to donate to Gates Foundation, 3000 letters from needy persons were received in his office. Everyday the letters were piling up. From-sick people, who did not have health insurance and could not afford their treatment; people injured during work and were unable to take care of their families; people whose children were suffering from incurable diseases and did not have sufficient funds left to carry on the treatment; helpless single mothers who had been left stranded by their lovers, at the mercy of God. Warren was sending all such letters to his sister Doris. For the last 10 years she had been managing the, 'Sunshine Lady Foundation' and helping persons affected by domestic violence. The foundation was being funded by, 'Howard Buffett Foundation'. The foundation had been aiding helpless families. Warren had also sent $ 5 million along with the letters.

Doris gave the responsibility of screening the letters to few women who more than 50 years old. Persons who had suffered due to bad luck, rather than by their own folly were given preference and due care was taken that it would possible to improve the circumstances of the affected persons with normal funding. She only offered advice to gamblers, debt ridden and lethargic persons. Also persons, who had alternatives to solve their problems, were not helped. Doris was also not in favour of fulfilling all needs. She said, "I don't want to become their mother." She also taught the people to write letters expressing their gratefulness. Who had received help, She wanted to inculcate the feeling of gratitude and self-esteem in them.

Warren was busy in managing billions of dollars of wealth. He had been donating $ 5 million every year to Ted Turner's campaign, 'Nuclear Threat Initiative' (N.T.I.). He believed that this was America's most powerful body, which working to strengthen global security by reducing global threats from nuclear, biological and chemical weapons. Warren wanted to give more help to this body. N.T.I. was being managed by former Senator Sam Nunn, who had suggested setting up an international bank for storing low-enriched uranium to address nuclear proliferation risks. Warren had liked the idea and offered to donate 50 million dollars and hoped that sufficient funds would be arranged for this campaign. Warren was ever ready to donate funds for nuclear non-proliferation campaigns. He was in favour of finding a permanent solution for this crisis.

Warren had extended financial help to the former US President Jimmy Carter to manage the activities of 'Carter Centre.' Carter, who departed from White House as an unpopular President, did not look back, nor was he discouraged. His contribution in the fields of health, democracy and human rights were considered remarkable and he was honoured with the, 'Noble Prize for Peace.' After receiving the donation from Warren, he wrote to him, "If you come to Ghana from 6th to 8th February, 2007, we shall be delighted. You can see the work being done by us." Warren considered Carter as his friend, but even his son and Gates could not convince him to undertake the plane journey to Ghana.

It was the 3rd time that he avoided travel to Africa. Some things do not change, but as time passes some things do change.

In the programs arranged outside Omaha, Astrid was accompanying Warren as his official life-partner. She had not changed at all, a frank person, idol of simplicity; but her life's circle was expanding rapidly. She regularly attended social functions along with Bill and Melinda Gates. In the winter of 2005, she travelled to Tahiti along with Warren, where Gates 50th birthday was going to be celebrated. It was being celebrated on Wall Allen's famous ship 'Octopus.' The ship had a movie theater and recording studio, two helicopters and a small submarine. Astrid and Warren's stay had been arranged at Allen's mother's magnificent house.

Overwhelmed by the hospitality extended by the world's 6th richest man, Astrid had remarked, "It was an amazing experience. I have never had such a magnificent experience earlier and maybe I shall never have it again in my life time."

According to Warren, the arrangements at sea were far better than they would been at home. They had returned after enjoying the bridge game.

Two years after Susie's death, on his 76th birthday, Warren married Astrid, in his daughter Susie Junior's house in a simple ceremony. In this function, only the family members were present. Astrid had worn a blouse and white pant while Warren was attired in a business suit. When Warren adorned Astrid's finger with a large sized diamond ring, tears trickled down from her eyes. After this they went out for dinner. Thereafter they reached San Francisco, where the marriage party had been arranged. The conventional marriage cake had been prepared at Sharon Osberg's home. The Gates couple was also present in the party.

Even though he was not an unsophisticated person, he started living a simple life. He had always wished to live a simple life. He had a wife, a car, a house which had not been renovated for years and a business. He started spending more time with his family.

Warren always used to say that a tree can never grow to reach the skies, but it can create new plants.

Warren's shareholders were wondering as to whom he will appoint as his successor. Warren used to make fun of this matter. It was definitely being felt that there can be no alternative to Warren. On one occasion he had said, "My ideas are fully ingrained in Berkshire." And people working with Berkshire and its investors were also ingrained with Warren's ideas.

Warren had once said if Berkshire continued to earn profit for its shareholder even 30 years after his death, then he will be happy. This was his thinking. The foundations of the organization which he had laid could service the next generation even in his absence. In fact, Warren was the soul of the structure and without him there could be a vacuum, which could not be filled up. Only Warren could take the decisions of the organization in the best way and an alternative to him could not even be imagined.

After Warren's death, the manner in which the shareholders of Berkshire will miss their CEO, perhaps in history no other group of shareholders will miss their CEO. No other group of shareholders must have considered their CEO as their mentor and friend, the way in which Warren's shareholders thought about him. The person who earned billions of dollars also won the hearts of thousands of persons. Such countless people used to consider him as their well-wisher, who had never met him personally. In spite of receiving countless letters from his admirers and signing autographs for them, Warren could not understand how much the people admired him or praised him. He would be elated like a teenager after receiving each letter. He would also be filled with happiness when someone asked for an autograph.

Even though trees could not reach the skies, Warren believed that they could help plants to grow. He retained his earlier focus towards his business; the moment he achieved would lead an ideal life, the preacher in him was awakened. He had started lecturing college students in America. He used to visit colleges or establish contact with them from Omaha. He liked to talk to students because they were like unbaked earthen pots, who could be motivated in the right direction.

He used to tell them that he had started making money very early in life. If he had delayed it by 10 years, then possibly he might not have attained such success. He advised them to start early and stay away from the credit card mentality.

In 2002, he increased his interactions with students. The students were coming from MIT, North Western, Iowa University, Nebraska University, Chicago University,

Indiana University, Michigan University, Houston University, Missouri University, Tennessee University and many educational institutions. He used to tell the students that the aim of becoming rich overnight was not important for living.

In 2008, he was declared as the richest man in the world. At that time students from Asian, Latin American and other countries started coming to Omaha. These students were extended excellent hospitality in Omaha.

The students asked more questions on subjects other than business, like what is the objective of life? The mathematical precision with which he replied to the questions related to business, he also replied to the other questions with the same adeptness.

When Susie was recovering in the hospital after her operation, then he had told the students from Georgia Institute of Technology about the purpose of life– "The purpose of life is to gain the love of the maximum number of persons from whom you wish to seek love."

To the question, how to get a perfect life-partner? He says, "Get married." To the question, what is right? He says, "Trust your heart." To the question, in which field should I make my career? He says, "The field is which you are passionate about." I work with people whom I like. The field in which you cannot apply your mind is not right for you."

Warren would say to the students- "Consider your body like a sole car which you have got for your entire life. Look after this car, park it in the garage in the night, remove all the stains, change oil regularly and so on." Then he used to take the students to a restaurant for lunch. After lunch, the students would have their photographs taken with Warren. Some day, maybe after 40 years, they could tell their grand-children about their meeting with Warren and having lunch with him. Warren was teaching them the mantras of life based on his lifelong experience.

During these discussions, he would accept that although he had great aspirations but he had made no plans from beginning to achieve them.

When Warren was very young and used to collect the crown caps, he had no inkling of what he was going to become. He distributed newspapers and he always ensured that they were delivered to the customers on time. If at that time had someone asked him whether he wanted to become the richest man in the world, then his heart would have replied - "Yes."

This dedication prompted him to study the world of share market. For hours, he would peruse such records in the library to which no one paid any attention. He would stay awake for nights and examine thousands of numbers to which no one else would have liked to pay any attention. Every morning he would read several newspapers thoroughly and would digest every word of, 'Wall Street Journal.' He would study the information on companies and would talk to their employees for hours. To understand the finer points of stocks, he would read magazines like 'Progressive Grocer.' When he went for his honeymoon, he carried copies of Moody's manual and Lesotho on the back seat of his car. For months he studied newspapers dating back to the last 100 years to understand the ups and downs in business, Wall Street's history, history of capitalism, history of modern Corporation's etc. He kept a close watch on the political events and tried to correlate its impact on business. He studied the economic parameters till he completely understood its implications. From his childhood, he had been studying the biographies of his favourite persons and kept learning lessons from their lives. He liked to be associated with people who could help him. He liked to keep his attention focused on the business world.

He had developed several skills to avoid making mistakes. He continuously thought about the different aspects of doing business– how to carry forward a good business? Why do businesses fail? What is competition? How to gain the trust of customers? He had a different way to find solutions for problems. He set up a network of loyal people who were always ready to help him with dedication. Whether the circumstances were favourable or adverse, he never stopped thinking about ways to create wealth.

Warren loved money. The game of accumulating wealth was into his blood flowing through his veins.

While celebrating his 77th birthday, he realized that possibly he has spent more than two thirds of his life on American soil. His age had started showing. It was now not possible for him to study for the whole day. The visibility in one eye was becoming hazy. His hearing was also getting impaired, so he agreed to wear hearing aids. He had also started speaking rapidly. He used to get tired soon. In spite of all this he was still capable of taking business decisions quickly and competently.

Warren's life's philosophy can be gauged from the following sentences– The snowball just happens if you're in the right kind of snow, and that's what happened with me. I don't just mean compounding money either. I did not wish to only expand my wealth to undreamed of levels, but wanted to explain it to the world and wanted to have a group of friends. You have to choose when the time comes. That's the way life works.

□

14

Charlie Munger and Warren Buffett

Charlie Thomas Munger had been working as the Vice-Chairman of Berkshire Hathaway along with Warren Buffett. Warren has often referred to him as his right hand man and partner. Warren had been telling that the extraordinary contribution made by Charlie, behind his success. He had an estimated net worth of $ 1.3 billion today.

Charlie was a lawyer earlier. He was given addmission to the Harvard Law School without a Bachelors degree, which was not an easy thing. Charlie was an exceptionally brilliant student and could easily answer complicated questions.

Warren met Charlie when he was practicing law in Omaha. Impressed by his personality, Warren asked him to leave his law practice and take up financial investing. Charlie consented. Time proved that Charlie's decision was correct.

Charlie was also the CEO of Wesco Financial Corporation, an associate company of Berkshire from 1984 to 2011. Like Warren, he also wrote annual letter to his shareholders through which one could learn useful tips of investing.

Charlie is not only a successful investor; he is also a

famous thinker who has been writing valuable quotes about business, investing and life in general.

Like Warren, Charlie is also from Omaha, Nebraska. After studies in Mathematics from University of Michigan and service in the US Army Air Corps as a meteorologist, trained at Caltech, he entered Harvard Law School.

Charlie is known by the world as Warren's associate; but he independently managed an investment partnership from 1962 to 1975. During this period the partnership generated compounded annual returns of 19.8 per cent, as compared to a 5 per cent annual appreciation for the Dow Jones Index.

Though Warren and Charlie are friends, there are lots of differences in their personalities. Charlie supports the Republican Party, whereas Warren is known to support the Democrats. Warren spends most of his time in managing the business, whereas Charlie likes to keep himself aloof from the day-to-day activities of the company. Charlie has been associated with different missions of philanthropy.

Charlie's principle is– "Good businesses are based on ethics. Businesses based on trickery are doomed to fail."

□

15

Warren's Ten Formulas to Earn Money

1. Invest the Profit

Drops make an Ocean. Even saving small amounts can turn into a big fortune. If you learn to save your profits then the magic of compound interest will keep on making you richer.

2. Don't Fall Into A Groove

Develop innovative thinking. Don't join the herd. Use your own wisdom for any investment. Don't invest on hearsay.

3. Avoid Doubt

People, who remain entrenched in doubt even loose golden opportunities. Take the decision to invest quickly after examining the available data.

4. Understand the Deal Before Deciding

Before taking any decision, understand the deal properly. Think carefully how it will profit you. It's like you must carefully read any document before signing.

5. Keep Minor Expenses Under Control

It's not as if only major expenses impact. Even minor

expenses can prove to be detrimental. Before incurring any expense, consider if it is justified.

6. Keep Debt Under Control

If you get into the habit of living on debit and credit card, then you can never become rich. By taking loan you can try to improve your living standard, but under the burden of debt, you will never be able to improve your financial state.

7. Maintain Continuity

If you think that the work being done by you is important and correct, then continue it. Keep advancing towards your goal with confidence.

8. Distance Yourself From Loss

If you feel that any investment is turning into a losing proposition, dispose it quickly. Sitting on it would lead to more loss.

9. Assess Risk

Before you decide to invest, think about the future consequences. You can take the right decision, after assessing the risks.

10. Understand the True Meaning of Success

For every person the meaning of success is different. Only accumulating money is not success. The things which give meaning to life, paying attention towards those things also as they are important components of success too. Out of those people whom you wished loved you and how many actually loves tells you the true meaning of success.

□

16

Warren Buffett's Seven Formulas Related to Happiness

1. Happiness Comes From Inside

"In my business career, I never felt the need to differentiate between professional and personal life. I get absorbed in my work and this gives me immense pleasure."

If you do the work of your choice, then your productivity also become better.

2. Look For Happiness In Ordinary Things

"I look for happiness in ordinary things. I play bridge online for 12 hours in a week." While playing with children, while wandering in natural environment, while talking to relations-friends, in all such small things, we can look for happiness.

3. Live Simply

"I only want to do such tasks, which have some significance. In my personal life I don't care about how other rich people are living in royal style. I don't want to buy a 405 feet long boat because some rich man has a 400 feet long boat."

4. Think Easy

"I am ready to accept my mistakes. This means that I undertake only those tasks, which I understand fully."

5. Invest Simply

"The best way to buy stocks is to invest in index funds."

6. Have A Mentor In Your Life

"I was lucky to get capable mentors. You tell me about your idol and I will tell you the direction in which your life will move. The persons whom you consider as your idols, practice their merits and imbibe them in your personality."

7. Earning Money is Not the Primary Objective of Life

"Earning money is not the primary objective of life; it is the by-product of your primary objective. If you love doing some work then you should get involved in it with full dedication. The process of earning money is also like that. Money should not be an achievement but a means."

□

17

Warren's Interest In India

The world's well-known investor Warren Buffett is quite impressed by India's fast growing economy. Warren feels that India offers unlimited business opportunities. He even believes that India's advancement can greatly benefit America. Keeping this in mind, he says that India can no longer be considered as a developing market. In other words, Indian market has developed to a large extent and it has become capable to provide new momentum to the economy of even a country like America.

In March 2011, Warren came to India for the first time. After his arrival, he told the reporters that he is looking for investment opportunities in large countries like India. He also said that he feels very happy, even if only one big investment idea succeeds in a year. So it does not matter that such an idea came from India or America or any other country. He thinks that the 26 per cent foreign investment limit in the insurance sector is not correct. Though there is a proposal to increase the investment limit to 49 per cent; not much progress is happening in that direction.

Warren only expressed his intention to invest in India but did not specify his plans. Warren, who is considered as the greatest warrior of investing, has invested in countries like China, Japan, Israel and South Korea in the past few years.

As far as India is concerned, Warren's company's presence is very small. His company Berkshire Hathaway has entered into an agreement with Bajaj Allianz to distribute motor insurance schemes. Recently they have formed a company called, 'Berkshire India', which has been appointed as their corporate agents for general insurance.

Even though Warren had come to India for expanding his mission's philanthropic activities, but he also perused at the possibilities of investing in India.

While touring India, he told the journalists that donating is harder than investing. The owner of $ 52 billion said that his needs are fulfilled with an annual salary of 100,000 dollars. I have no use for the rest of it, so it will be given back to the society.

Indicating the possibility of appointing an Indian as his successor, Warren said that he is thankful to India for giving him Ajit Jain. He said that Ajit Jain is more capable than him.

□

18

Warren Buffett's Quotes

(Leaking Boat)

Should you find yourself in a chronically leaking boat. Great managers should devote their energy to changing vessels; it is likely to be more productive than energy devoted to patching leaks.

(Buffett on Lou Simpson)

Temperament is what causes smart people not to function well. His temperament probably isn't different than mine. We both tend to do rational things. Our emotions don't get in the way of our intellect.

(Charlie Munger)

His portfolio was concentrated in a very few securities and therefore his record was much more volatile but it was based on the same discount-from-value approach. He was willing to accept greater peaks and valleys of performance, and he happens to be a fellow whose whole psyche focuses on concentration.

Our capital is not fully invested. Our positing is disturbing, but not as much, as it would have been, had we taken a foolish decision.

(Invest in Korea when the dollar is strong and the Korean companies cheaper).

They make basic things like– steel, cement, flour and electricity, which people will continue to buy for the next 10 years. They have a big presence in the Korean market, which is unlikely to change. The flour mills cash valuation is much higher than its market valuation, and its sales are 3 times of its earning.

(On Profit)

Before you decide on how to deploy your cash, it is essential that you assess four simple common sense questions based on information, instead of deciding on rumours. The events occurrence possibility, for how long the fund will remain invested, the expenses which will be incurred and a negative aspect– what happens if the event does not take place?

(On being asked what is his next target, after becoming America's richest man).

This is easy– become America's oldest man.

(On Managing Risk)

Spend as much time, as was spent on strengthening the New Orleans's Dam before the onset of cyclone Catarina.

(On the Stock Market)

Don't be scared of the ups and downs. Don't buy and sell. Don't get trapped in that stuff. Don't look at the newspaper everyday.

After some time there will be only a few companies left which will of that standard. So when you find a company of that standard, then you should buy a reasonable quantity of its stock. You must save yourself from the temptation of straying away from your path. If you want a stock for the next 10 years, then don't even think of buying it for 10 minutes.

(Value Investor)

These are investors, who mentally buy a business, not stock. But everyone gains from the difference between actual value and the market price.

(Warren On Wealth)

It made me independent. Then I did in life what I wanted to do. The thing which I wanted to do most was to be self-employed. I did not want that others direct me. I should be able to do what I wanted to do everyday; this thought was important for me.

A by-product of our managerial style is the ability it gives us to easily expand Berkshire's activities. We've read management treatises that specify exactly how many people should report to any one executive, but they make little sense to us. When you have able managers of high character running businesses about which they are passionate, you can have a dozen or more reporting to you and still have time for an afternoon nap. Conversely, if you have even one person reporting to you who is deceitful, inept or uninterested, you will face so many difficulties that it will be hard to resolve them. Charlie and I could work with double the number of managers we have now, so long as they had the rare qualities of the present ones.

It's far better to buy a wonderful company at a fair price than a fair company at a wonderful price. You get great opportunities for investing, when excellent companies face abnormal circumstances, which suppresses their price.

In the world several persons have attained lucky heights through one excellent business. If you understand your business then you don't need to buy several businesses.

A man who tries to carry a cat home by its tail will learn a lesson that can't be learned in any other way.

A parent company that owns a subsidiary with superb long-term economics will not sell the company's, 'crown jewel'. Yet this same CEO will impulsively sell stocks in his personal portfolio with little more logic than, 'You can't go broke by taking a profit'. In our view what makes sense in business also makes sense in stocks. An investor should ordinarily hold a small piece of an outstanding business with the same tenacity that an owner would exhibit if he owned all of that business.

A partner who does not accept your command is extremely argumentative and is like a superlative charm for you.

A public survey cannot take the place of original ideas.

A stock doesn't know that you own it.

A stock makes you an owner of a business and you had assessed its inherent value; but if your profit is not protected then you cannot sleep peacefully at night.

While investing you must take care that you buy good stocks at the right time and retain them till the companies continue to perform.

Always do the thing, what you wish to do.

Americans are trapped in a fear psychosis which restrains them from spending or investing. This enhances their fear even more. We have to break this vicious circle, but it takes time.

An investor needs to do a very few things right in life so long as he doesn't do too many things wrong.

And after that I changed my war strategy and instead of buying a right business at a good price, I tried to buy a good business at the right price.

Any person, who does not play bridge, is making a big mistake.

As one of the Indianapolis '500' winners said: 'To finish first in the race, you must first finish the race'.

We rejected many opportunities for mergers and buying, which would have increased many fold our current and short-term profit. But that would have reduced the intrinsic value of Berkshire Hathaway's share. Instead we have been following Wayne Gretzky's viewpoint which says that you should go where the devil is about to go and not where he already is.

Basically, when you get to my age, you'll really measure your success in life, by how many of the people you want to have love you, actually do love you. I know people who have a lot of money. They attend appreciation letter dinners and build hospital wings named after them. But the fact is that nobody in the world loves them. When you attain my age and nobody thinks well about you, then it does not matter how much money you have in your account, your life is ruined. This is the final test of how you have lived your life. The trouble with love is that you cannot buy it. You can buy self-praising leaflets. The only way to get love is to be lovable. It's very irritating if you have a lot of money. You'd like to think you could write a check: 'I'll buy a million dollars' worth of love.' But it doesn't work that way. The more you give love away, the more you get.

Be satisfied with average profits also.

Be fearful when others are greedy and be greedy only when others are fearful.

Benjamin Graham rightly says that the share market is eccentric. That's why you cannot buy or sell its (market's) terms. You can buy or sell, whenever you wish to do so.

Berkshire Hathaway buys when Lomings is not buying.

Berkshire has access to two low-cost, non-perilous sources of leverage that allows us to safely own far more assets than our equity capital alone would permit: deferred taxes and 'float', the funds of others that our insurance business holds because it receives premiums before needing to pay out losses. Both of these funding sources have grown rapidly and now total about $77 billion. Better yet, this funding to date has been cost-free. Deferred tax liabilities bear no interest. And as long as we can break even in our insurance underwriting - which we have done on average, during our 29 years in the business - the cost of the float developed from that operation is zero. Neither item– it should be understood is equity; these are real liabilities. But they are liabilities without covenants or due dates attached to them. In fact, they give us the benefit of debt - an ability to have more assets working for us - but saddle us with none of its drawbacks.

Beware of greek bearing formulas.

Once Warren was found picking up a one cent coin in a lift. He told the surprised persons, "This is the beginning of my next billion."

Weak and insecure businesses cannot make good investments.

As it happens frequently in Wall Street, what the wise do in the beginning, the fools do it in the end.

Every time Stan Perlmeter bought a stock was because he was getting more for his money than he was paying. In other words, he was buying $1 for less than $1 -- the underlying principle of deep value investing. Stan Perlmeter wasn't concerned about quarterly earnings projections or even next year's earnings projections. He didn't care which Wall Street brokers had a buy recommendation on the stock or a sell recommendation. He wasn't interested in price momentum, volume, or anything. He was simply asking: What is the business worth?

Can you really explain to a fish what it's like to walk on the land? One day on land is worth a thousand years of talking about it, and the cost of running a business for a day is exactly the same.

In a crisis, the combination of cash and courage is priceless.

Chains of habit are too light to be left until they are too heavy to be broken.

Change, which happened due to internet can be society-friendly. But it is the lack of change which befriends an investor. Internet will change a lot of things. But it cannot change chewing gum's brand, which people chew. Charlie and I want a stable business like chewing gum and want to leave the life's unexpected things for others.

Charlie and I have not learnt how to solve the business problems. What we have learnt is how to avoid them.

Charlie and I know that the right players will make almost any team manager look good. We subscribe to the philosophy of Ogilvy and Mather's founding genius, David Ogilvy: "If each of us hires people who are smaller than we are, we shall become a company of dwarfs. But, if each of us hires people who are bigger than we are, we shall become a company of giants.

Charlie and I pay special attention to how well our business is doing; we also try to understand the circumstances in which our business is running. For example, is any of our business following the industry's trend or going against it? Charlie and I want to know the situation and we mould our expectations accordingly.

Charlie and I were introduced in 1959 by the Davis family. We were two personalities who tended towards dominance. Yet, we've never had an argument since.

Charlie can analyse and evaluate any kind of deal faster and more accurately than any person in the world. He sees any valid weakness in 60 seconds. He is a perfect partner.

Charlie taught me to focus on the merits of the business with tremendously growing earning power, but only when you can be sure of it - not like Texas Instruments or Polaroid, where earning potential was hypothetical.

Charlie Munger, our Vice-Chairman and I really have only two jobs. One is to attract and keep outstanding managers to run our various operations; the other one is capital allocation. This hasn't been all that difficult. Usually the managers came with the companies we bought, having demonstrated their talents throughout careers that spanned a wide variety of business circumstances. They were managerial stars long before they knew us, and our main contribution has been not to get in their ways. This approach seems elementary: if my job were to manage a golf team and if Jack Nicklaus or Arnold Palmer were willing to play for me - neither would get a lot of directives about how to swing from me.

Charlie says as you get older, you tolerate more and more in your old friends and less, and less in your new friends.

Charlie led me in a new direction which went beyond buying at cheap prices as Benjamin Graham had taught me. He really influenced me. I needed a powerful force to move away from Graham's limited outlook. This power came from Charlie's brain. He expanded the outlook.

Derivatives are financial weapons of mass destruction.

Variety is a protection against ignorance. But it is of no use to people who know what they are doing.

Doing little can earn more profits.

Don't bet; be on the lookout for abnormal circumstances. The best time to invest comes when top notch businesses face circumstances, which reduces their share prices below their intrinsic value.

Don't look back or don't regret.

Don't buy a share for 10 minutes if you are not ready to buy it for 10 years.

Do not risk what is important for you, for the sake of what is not important for you.

The remedy for the economy which was earlier served in a cup, is now being served in a barrel. The doses which were not even conceived earlier are bound to cause undesirable effects. Even though no one can predict its correct effects, an inevitable outcome will be unbridled inflation.

Everyone who praises himself will become a pauper and the pauper shall be praised.

First, each pair is stronger than the sum of its parts because each partner understands, trusts and admires the other. Second, both managerial teams pay capable people well, but abhor having a bigger headcount than needed. Third, both attack costs as vigorously when profits are at record levels, as when they are under pressure. Finally both stick with what they understand and let their abilities, not their egos, determine what they attempt. Thomas J Watson of IBM followed the same rule: He said, "I am no genius. I am smart in spots - but I stay around those spots."

Follow Graham and instead of committing a mistake you will profit from it.

Forecasts may tell you a great deal about the forecaster; they tell you nothing about the future.

Frankly, airlines can never turn into a good business.

Good investment ideas are rare, valuable and subject to competitive appropriation just as good product or business acquisition ideas are.

Normally a decent profit is not inconsistent with a good behaviour.

Graham's teachings have made a number of people rich, and it is difficult to find any cases where those teachings have made anyone poor. There are not many men about whom you can say that.

Happiness comes from small improvements, not by getting somewhere once and for all. Being able to add on one room to your house is what makes you happy, not living in a palace.

I always knew that I am going to be rich; I don't think I doubted it for a minute. There was Western Insurance earning sixteen dollars a share, and selling at sixteen dollars a share. There was National Insurance selling at one time's earnings. How could it miss?

I am a better investor because I am a businessman and I am a better businessman because I am an investor.

I am a big bull in this country. We shall never dip in the slow down twice. I see my business reviving from all angles.

I am likely to limit myself to things which are reasonably easy, safe, profitable and give happiness.

I seriously say that nowhere else in the world, there are so many sharp holes as in America. No person will properly understand the meaning of this word, unless he comes here.

I ate lunch in the Omaha Club - that's the Downtown Club - and I noticed there weren't any Jews. I was told, 'They have their own club'. Now there are Jewish families that have contributed to the community all the time, they have helped build Omaha as much as anybody, and yet they can't join a club that John Jones, the new middle rank Union Pacific Man, joins as soon as he is transferred here. That is hardly fair. So I joined the Jewish Club; it took me four months - they were a little put back and confused, and I had to do some convincing. Then I went back to the Omaha Club and told them that the Jewish Club wasn't totally Jewish any more. I got two or three of the Jewish Club members to apply to the Omaha Club. Now we've eliminated the restrictions.

I buy expensive suits. They just look cheap on me.

I can't think of anything in life I want, that I don't have.

I could improve your ultimate financial welfare by giving you a ticket with only twenty slots in it so that you had twenty punches - representing all the investments that you get to make in a lifetime. And once you'd punched through the card, you couldn't make any more investments at all. Under those rules, you'd really think carefully about what you did, and you'd be forced to load up on what you'd really thought about. So you'd do so much better.

I never value my life with the money I have earned. Others might do it, but I never do it.

I don't try to jump over seven-foot bars; I just look around for one-foot bars that I can step over.

I feel like an oversexed guy in a harem. This happens when I start investing.

I have never met a man who could forecast the market.

I have done value investing for 35 years but I have never seen a trend. There seems to be some perverse human characteristic that likes to make easy things difficult.

I only think that when we and a country needs more money, then we calculate that the GDP should rise by 15 per cent. What I mean to say that when a country needs more money, then they should take it from the people who are wealthy.

I learned that it pays to hang around with people better than you are, because you will float upward a little bit. And if you hang around with people who are worse than you, pretty soon you'll start sliding down the pole. It just works that way.

I like a business which I can predict where it will be after 5 or 10 or 15 years. I know where Coke will be.

I like people who sell their business to me and continue to operate it as if they were still its owners. It's like I marry my daughter and she continues to stay with her parents.

I like to work in Berkshire Hathaway for a few simple reasons– it generates a sense of achievement in me; it gives me the freedom to do as I wish; and everyday it gives me a chance to talk to people whom I like and trust.

I never attempt to make money on the stock market. I buy on the assumption that they could close the market the next day and not reopen it for five years. As far as you are concerned, the stock market does not exist. Ignore it. Much success can be attributed to inactivity. Most investors cannot resist the temptation to constantly buy and sell.

I never talk to brokers or analysts. Wall Street is the only place where people who ride to work in a Rolls Royce get advice from those who take the subway.

I read the annual report of my company and I also read the annual report of my competitor's companies. They are the main source of information.

I read the first edition of this book (The Intelligent Investor), in early 1950 when I was about nineteen. I thought then it was by far the best book about investing ever written. I still think it is.

I really like my life. I've arranged my life so that I can do what I want.

I understand the most important factor which helped us to recover from slowdown resurrection capacity of American capitalism.

I want to explain my mistakes. This means I do only the things I completely understand.

I went the whole way. I collected charts and I read all the technical stuff. I listened to tips. And then I picked up Graham's Security Analysis. It was like a revelation to me.

I would rather have a $10 million business making 15% than a $100 million business making 5%.

If the markets were always efficient, I would have been roaming on the streets like a mad cap with a tin cup.

I'll be happy to accept a lottery ticket as a gift - but I'll never buy one.

I'm convinced that there is much inefficiency in the market. These Graham-and-Doddsville investors have successfully exploited gaps between price and value.

I'm not competent to judge his (Bill Gates) technical ability but I regard his business savvy as extraordinary. If Bill had started a hot dog stand, he would have become the hot dog king of the world. He will win in any game. He would be very good at my business, but I wouldn't be at his.

Till now, I have not a person who has over a period of 10 years gradually accepted this viewpoint. It has nothing to do with IQ or educational training. It is a matter of instant recall or nothing.

If a business does well, its share also do well.

If a company's future cannot be predicted, it cannot be valued.

If a graduating MBA were to ask me, 'How do I get rich in a hurry?' I would not respond with quotations from Ben Franklin or Horatio Alger, but would, instead, hold my nose with one hand and point with the other towards Wall Street.

If nothing else, then for the lower and middle classes, and if possible for the upper middle class, the tax should be further reduced. But I think that for people like me who are sitting on a high pedestal, should pay more taxes. Our position is better than before, like never before.

If Fed Chairman Alan Greenspan were to whisper to me what his monetary policy was going to be over the next two years, it wouldn't change one thing I do.

If the concept doesn't attract a person right away, I find that you can talk to him for years and show him records and it doesn't make any difference. They just don't seem able to grasp the concept, simple as it is.

If it is not important or worth knowing then don't bother about it.

If principles can become dated, they're not principles.

If someone goes through life and value themselves solely by how much they have, or how much money they earned last year, sooner or later they're going to end up in trouble.

If you are going to drive 10,000 pound truck across a bridge repeatedly, it is well to build one that can withstand 15,000 pound load rather than one that can withstand

10,000 pounds. It is a big mistake to have lots of financial obligations and no cash reserve. Personally, I have never used more than 25% borrowed money in my life, including when I had only $10,000 and had ideas that made me wish I had $100 million.

If you believe your gain after considering the probabilities, if your gain considerably exceeds your loss, comparably weighed then you are consciously going for a risky investment.

If you cannot control your emotions, you cannot control your money.

If you give me $100 million and tell me to take away the soft drink leadership of Coca-Cola in the world, I'd give it back to you and say it can't be done.

If you understand a business, you need not have many of them.

In a business selling commodity products, it's impossible to be a lot smarter than your dumbest competitor.

In my opinion, investment success will not be achieved by arcane formulae, computer programs or signals flashed by the price behaviour of stocks and markets. Rather an investor will succeed by combining good business judgment with an ability to insulate his thoughts and behaviour from the super-contagious emotions that abound the marketplace. In my own efforts to stay insulated, I have found it highly useful to keep Ben's Mr. Market concept firmly in mind.

In the 20th century, United States of America faced two world wars and underwent painful and expensive armed conflicts. It experienced dozens of slowdowns, financial turmoil, oil crisis, flu, epidemic and resignation of a tainted President. Yet the Dow Jones Industrial Index moved up from 66 to 11,497.

In the business world you get a clearer view in the rear view than the front wind screen.

In the end, I always believe my eyes rather than anything else.

In the short run, the market is a voting machine. In the long run, it's a weighing machine.

Indeed, if you aren't certain that you understand and can value your business far better than Mr. Market then you are not fit for this game.

Investing is about the study of human nature.

Investing is not a game where the guy with the 160 IQ beats the guy with the 130 IQ.

Investing is simple but not easy.

Investment is an activity of forecasting the yield on assets over the life of the asset. Speculation is the activity of forecasting the psychology of the market.

Investment must be rational. If you can't understand it, don't do it.

It baffles us how many people know of Ben Graham but so few follow. We tell our principles freely and write about them extensively in our annual reports. They are easy to learn. They should be easy to follow. But the only thing anyone wants to know is, 'What we are buying today?' Like Graham, we are widely recognised but least followed.

It has been helpful to me to have tens of thousands (of students) turned out of business schools who have been taught that it didn't do any good to think.

It is not necessary to do extraordinary things to get extraordinary results.

It is not that we don't understand a technology business or its product. The reason we don't invest is because we can't understand the predictability of the economics ten years hence.

It takes 20 years to build a reputation and five minutes to gain notoriety. If you think about it then you will do things differently.

It's easier to create money than to spend it.

It's much easier to stay out of trouble now than to get out of trouble later.

It's not that I want money. It's the fun of making money and watching it grow.

It's only when the tide goes out that you learn who had been swimming naked.

It's good to spend time with people who are better than you. Choose those colleagues whose behaviour is better than yours and you will also improve your behaviour.

It never helps to bet against America. We pass through a lot of situations but this journey is never easy.

Let only fools read what fools write.

Treat the fluctuations of the market as a friend and not as an enemy; instead of slipping, use is to your advantage.

Look first for someone both smarter and wiser than you are. After locating him (or her) ask him not to flaunt his superiority so that you may enjoy acclaim for the many accomplishments that sprang from his thoughts and advice. Seek a partner who will never second-guess you nor sulk when you make expensive mistakes. Look also for a generous soul who will put up his own money and work for peanuts. Finally, join with someone who will constantly add to the fun as you travel a long road together.

Managers and investors alike must understand that accounting numbers are the beginning, not the end of business valuation.

Managers eager to bet heavily on their abilities usually have plenty of ability to bet upon.

Managers of the Berkshire subsidiaries are worth, on average $100 million. They all love what they are doing. Otherwise, they would retire, since they are no longer working for money.

Maybe grapes from a little eight acre vineyard in France are really the best in the world, but I always had a suspicion that about 99 per cent of it is in the telling and about 1 per cent of it is in the drinking.

Money is a by-product of doing something I like doing extremely well.

Money will not change how healthy you are or how many people love you.

Money, to some extent, sometimes let you be in more interesting environments. But it can't change how many people love you or how healthy you are.

Most business owners spend the better part of their lifetimes building their businesses. By experience built upon endless repetition, they sharpen their skills in merchandising, purchasing, personnel etc. It's a learning process and mistakes made in one year often contribute to competence and success in the subsequent years.

Most of our managers are independently wealthy, and it's, therefore, up to us to create a climate that encourages them to choose working with Berkshire over golfing or fishing.

Most people get interested in stocks when everyone else is. The time to get interested is when no one else is. You can't buy what is popular and become rich.

Mr. Market is there to serve you, not to guide you. It will be disastrous if you fall under his influence.

Madam B (Blumkin) had a native genius which consisted of staying focused on the one area of her expertise.

My biggest mistakes are the investments which I did not make.

My conclusion from my own experiences and from in-depth study of other businesses is that a good managerial record (measured by economic returns), is far more a function of what business boat you get into than it is of how effectively you row (though intelligence and effort help considerably, of course in any business good or bad). Some years ago I wrote: 'When a management with a reputation for brilliance tackles a business with a reputation for poor fundamental economics, it is the reputation of the business that remains intact.' Nothing has since changed my point of view on the matter. Should you find yourself in a chronically leaking boat energy devoted to changing vessels is likely to be more productive than energy devoted to patching leaks.

My job is to keep a group of 15-20 managers enthused about what they are doing, because most of them are already wealthy beyond their beliefs.

Never ask a barber whether you need a haircut.

Never lie under any circumstances. Don't pay any attention to the lawyers. If you start letting lawyers get into the picture, they'll basically tell you, 'Don't say anything.' You'll never get tangled up if you just state what you have seen truthfully.

From the billionaires whom I know, money only brings out their inner characteristics. If they were fools before becoming wealthy, then even after making billions of dollars they will ordinarily continue to be fools.

One important thing about risk and reward-sometimes risk and reward are correlated in a positive fashion. If someone were to say to me, 'I have here a six-shooter and I have slipped one cartridge into it. Why don't you just spin it and pull it once? If you survive, I will give you $1 million.' I would decline –perhaps stating that $1 million is not enough. Then he might offer me $5 million to pull the trigger twice – now that would be a positive correlation between risk and reward! The exact opposite is true with value investing. If you buy a dollar bill for 60 cents, it's riskier than if you buy a dollar bill for 40 cents, but the expectation of reward is greater in the latter case. The greater the potential for reward in the value portfolio, the less risk there is.

One lesson is not to overly fixate on what you have paid for a stock, the second is not to rush unthinkingly and grab a small profit.

One of the things that attracted me to work with securities was the fact that you could live your own life. You don't have to worry about success.

Buy only what you would be happy to retain even if the market is closed for 10 years.

Our (investment) attitude fits our personalities and the way we want to live our lives.

Our favourite holding period is forever.

Our goal is to find an outstanding business at a sensible price, not a mediocre business at a bargain price.

People always want a formula – but it doesn't always work that way. You have to estimate total cash generated from now to eternity, and discount it back to today. Yardsticks such as P/E's are not enough by themselves.

People who buy for non-value reasons are likely to sell for non-value reasons. Their presence in the picture will accentuate erratic price swings, unrelated to business developments.

People would rather be promised a (presumably) winning lottery ticket next week than an opportunity to get rich slowly.

Philanthropy is harder than business. You are tackling important problems that people with intellect and money have tackled in the past and had a tough time solving. So the search for talent in philanthropy should be even more important than the search for talent in investments, where the game is not as tough.

Philosophically, I am in the elderly ward. We live in an investment world populated not by those who must be logically persuaded to believe, but by the hopeful, credulous and greedy, grasping for an excuse to believe.

Praise by name, criticise by category.

Price fluctuations are there to provide opportunity to buy wisely when prices fall sharply, other times you would do better to forget the market and pay attention to the operating results of companies.

Price is what you pay, value is what you get.

Regardless of price, we have no interest at all, in selling any good businesses that Berkshire owns, and are very reluctant to sell sub-par businesses - even if that hurts performance - as long as we expect them to generate at least some cash and as long as we feel good about their managers and labour relations.

Retirement plans? About 5 to 10 years after I die.

Risk comes from not knowing what you are doing.

Risk is a part of God's game– it is same for people and countries.

Investing Rule Number 1: Never lose money. Investing Rule Number 2: Never forget Rule Number 1. Investing Rule Number 3: Don't get trapped in debt.

Several years ago Ben Graham, then almost eighty, expressed to a friend the thought that he hoped everyday to do 'something foolish (whimsical), something creative and something generous.

Size is the anchor of performance.

So we think in terms of that moat and the ability to keep its width and its impossibility of being crossed as the primary criterion of a great business. And we tell our managers that we want the moat widened every year. That doesn't necessarily mean the profit will be more this year than it was last year because it sometimes won't be. However, if the moat is widened every year, the business will do very well. When we see a moat that's tenuous in any way – it's just too risky. We don't know how to evaluate that. And, therefore, we leave it alone. We think that all of our businesses – or virtually all of our businesses – have pretty good moats. And we think our managers are widening them.

Some of our key managers are independently wealthy (we hope they all become so), but that poses no threat to their continued interest: they work because they love what they do and relish the thrill of outstanding performance.

They unfailing think like owners (the highest compliment we can pay a manager), and find all aspects of their business absorbing.

Somebody once said that in looking for people to hire, you look for three qualities: integrity, intelligence, and energy. And if they don't have the first, the other two will kill you. You think about it; it's true. If you hire somebody without the first, you really want them to be dumb and lazy.

Someone is sitting under the shade today because someone planted a tree a long time ago.

Speculation is most dangerous when it looks easiest.

Continue to invest in your sphere of competence.

IQ has nothing to do with investing once you cross the level of 25. Once you attain average intelligence, then you need a frame of mind, which can rein the impulsiveness on account of which other people get into trouble after investing.

The ability to raise prices – the ability to differentiate yourself in a real way, and the real way means you can charge a different price – makes a great business.

Business schools reward complicated and difficult behaviour over normal behaviour, but normal behaviour is more effective.

A dominant retailer in first twenty-years is not necessarily going to be the dominant retailer in the coming years.

The world's most foolish person is one who buys shares when its price is rising.

The fact that people will be full of greed, fear or folly is predictable. The sequence is not predictable.

The financial calculus that Charlie and I employ would never permit our trading, a good night's sleep for a shot, at a few extra percentage points of return. I've never believed in risking what my family and friends have and need in order to pursue what they don't have and don't need.

The first step to earning profit is to stop doing the wrong thing.

The future is never clear. You pay a very high price in the stock market for a joyful consensus. Uncertainty is the long-term buyer's friend.

The inescapable fact is that the value of an asset, whatever it's character, cannot over the long-term, grow faster than its earnings.

Today's investor does not capitalise on yesterday's gains.

The key is having more information than the other person or the competitor – then it should be analysed correctly and use rationally.

The market is there only as a reference point to see if anybody is going to do something foolish. When we invest in stocks, we invest in businesses.

The most common cause of low prices is pessimism – sometimes all pervasive, sometimes specific to a company or industry. We want to do business in such an environment, not because we like pessimism but because we like the prices it produces. It's optimism that is the enemy of the rational buyer.

The right time to buy them (shares) is when no one else is buying.

The only value of stock forecasters is to make fortune tellers look good. The purpose of life is to be loved by as many people as possible, out of those whom you want should love you.

The rich will always say, you understand, give us more money and you will get more and you will be able to spend it and it will gradually reach you. But for the last 10 years it is not working and I hope that the American people will now get a grip on it.

The secret of making money is to avoid risks; you take risks when you spend it.

The sign above the players' entrance to the field at Notre Dame reads, 'Play like a champion today'. I sometimes joke that the sign at Nebraska reads. 'Remember your helmet'. Charlie and I are 'Remember your helmet', kind of guys. We like to keep it simple.

The sillier is the market's behaviour, the greater the opportunity for business-like investing.

The smarter the journalists, the better is the society; because to some extent people read newspapers for information. And the better the teachers, the better the performance of students.

The smartest side to take in a bidding war is the losing side.

The snowball just happens if you're in the right kind of snow, and that's what happened with me. I don't just mean compounding money either. It's in terms of understanding the world and what kind of friends you accumulate. You get to select over time, and you've got to be the kind of person that the snow wants to attach itself to. You've got to be your own wet snow, in effect. You'd better be picking up snow as you go along, because you're not going to be getting back up to the top of the hill again. That's the way life works.

The stock market is not a strike game. You don't have to swing at everything – you can wait for your pitch. The problem is when you're a money manager, your fans keep yelling, 'Swing your bums.'

The stock market serves as a relocation centre at which money moves from the impatient person to the patient person.

The trick is, when there is nothing to do, do nothing.

The way to wealth is as plain as the road to the supermarket. It depends on two words industriousness and stinginess.

There are 309 million people who want to reincarnate their lives; we have the technique which makes it possible for them to do it.

There are always people who say that the rules have changed. But it only looks that way, if the time horizon is too short.

There are certain kinds of businesses where you have to be smart once and the kind where you have to stay smart everyday to defend it. Retailing is one of them. If you find a retailing concept that catches on, you have to defend it everyday.

There is also another alternative: Don't do anything. More fortunes are made by sitting on good securities for years at a time than by active trading.

There seems to be some perverse human characteristic that likes to make easy things difficult.

This is the cornerstone of our investment philosophy: Never count on making a good sale. Have the purchase be so attractive that even a mediocre sale gives good results.

Those who read their Graham and Dodd will continue to prosper.

Thus our first lesson: businesses logically are worth far more than net tangible assets when they are expected to produce earnings on such assets considerably in excess of market rates of return. The capitalised value of this excess return is economic goodwill.

Time is the friend of the wonderful business, the enemy of the mediocre. You might think this principle is obvious, but I had to learn it the hard way… It is far better to buy a wonderful company at a fair price than a fair company at a wonderful price. Charlie understood this early; I was a slow learner. But now, when buying companies or common stocks, we look for first class businesses accompanied by first class managements. That leads right into a related lesson: Good jockeys will do well on good horses, but not on lamed ones.

To invest successfully over a lifetime, does not require a stratospheric IQ, unusual business insights, or inside information. What's needed is a sound intellectual framework for making decisions and the ability to keep emotions from corroding that framework. This book (The Intelligent Investor) precisely and clearly prescribes the proper framework. You must maintain emotional discipline.

To some, our stand may seem highly eccentric. Charlie and I have long followed David Ogilvy's advice: 'Develop your eccentricities while you are young. That way, when you get old, people won't think you have lost your mind.'

To swim a fast 100 metres, it's better to swim with the tide than to work on your stroke.

Today people, who hold their wealth in cash, feel at ease. They should not do so. They will own this wealth for dangerously long periods of time; it will not yield anything and it is bound to depreciate.

Tom Murphy started managing a bankrupt TV station in Albany, so frugally that he painted only the sides of the building that faced the road.

Upon my death, Berkshire's earnings will immediately increase by $1 million, since Charlie will sell the corporate jet the next day, ignoring my wish to be buried with the indefensible.

Valuing a business is partly Art and part Science.

Walter Lippmann spoke of men who plant trees that other men will sit under. Ben Graham was such a man.

We live in a perennially uncertain world. But it is certain that United States of America will keep on progressing with time.

We understand that amongst the companies actively involved in business, these names are somewhat like calling a call girl's one night stand as romantic.

We continually look for ways to employ large sums in each area. But we try to avoid small commitments. If something's not doing well, it's not worth doing at all.

We diversify substantially less than most investment operations. We might invest up to 40% of our net worth in a single security under conditions, coupling an extremely high probability that our facts and our reasoning are correct with a very low probability that anything could drastically change the underlying value of the investment.

We do not have, ever had, and never will have an opinion about where the stock market, interest rates, or business activity will be a year from now.

We don't get into things, we don't understand. We buy very few things, but we buy very big positions. Know what you own, own a few and buy a lot.

We don't get paid for activity, just for being right. As to how long we'll wait, we'll wait indefinitely.

We don't get paid for activity; we get paid for being right.

We enjoy the activity more than the results.

We find it hard to teach a new dog, old tricks. But we haven't had lots of problems with people who hit the ball out of the park, year after year. Even though they're rich, they love what they do. And nothing ever happens to our managers. We offer them immortality.

We have carefully designed both the company and our jobs so that we do things we enjoy with people we like. Equally important, we are forced to do very few boring or unpleasant tasks.

We intend to continue our practice of working only with people whom we like and admire. This policy not only maximises our chances for good results, it also ensures us an extraordinarily good time. On the other hand, working with people who cause your stomach to churn seems much like marrying for money – probably a bad idea under any circumstances, but absolute madness if you are already rich.

We train our sights on only a few excellent companies.

We like to buy businesses; we don't like to sell them.

We not only encourage extraordinary autonomy in our operating businesses, we also rely on them.

We rarely use much debt and when we do, we attempt to structure it on a long-term fixed rate basis. We will reject interesting opportunities rather than over-leverage our balance sheet.

We regard our (Insurance) float as a very significant asset.

We select our marketable equity securities in much the same way as we would evaluate a business for acquisition in its entirety. We want the business to be one, a) that we understand, b) with favourable long-term prospects, c) operated by honest and competent people and d) available at a very attractive price.

We want managers who tell the truth, and they believe in the truth – which is more important.

We want people who think of themselves as business owners and invest in companies with the intention of staying a long time. And we like people who keep their eyes focused on business results, not market prices.

We will continue to ignore political and economic forecasts, which are an expensive distraction for many investors and businessmen. Thirty years ago, no one could have foreseen the huge expansion of the Vietnam War, wage and price controls, two oil shocks, the resignation of a President, the dissolution of the Soviet Union, a one-day drop of 508 points in the Dow, or treasury bill yields fluctuating between 2.8% and 17.4%. Imagine the cost to us. If we had let fear of unknowns, to defer or alter the deployment of capital. Indeed, we have usually made our best purchases when apprehensions about some macro event were at a peak. Fear is the foe of the happy go lucky, but the friend of the fundamentalist.

We will stick with the approach that got us here and try not to relax our standards. Ted Williams in, "The story of my life" explains why: 'My argument is to be a good hitter; you've got to get a good ball to hit. It's the first rule in the book. If I have to bite at stuff that is out of my happy zone, I'm not a .344 hitter. I might only be a .250 hitter.' Charlie and I agree and will try to wait for opportunities that are well within our own, 'happy zone'.

We're not in the steel business. We're not in the shoe business. We're not in any business. We're big in insurance, but we're not committed to it. We don't have a mindset that says you have to go down this road. So we can take capital and move it into businesses that makes sense.

We are now in a depression. We may not get out of it for some more time, but we will certainly come out of it.

We have used several bullets and we are talking about encouragement. But the fact is that we had a deficit of 9 per cent of the GDP. It is an encouragement that we recovered. It is much more encouraging than any other policy which we have implemented after the Second World War.

What could be more exhilarating than to participate in a bull market in which the, 'Rewards to the owners of the business become gloriously uncoupled from the plodding performance of the businesses themselves'. Unfortunately however, stocks can't outperform businesses indefinitely.

What counts for most people investing is not how much they know, but rather how realistically they define what they don't know. Paradoxically when dumb money acknowledges its limitations, it ceases to be dumb.

What we do is not beyond anybody else's competence. It is just not necessary to do extraordinary things to get extraordinary results.

What's the sense in getting rich just to stare at the ticker tape all day?

When a management with a reputation for brilliance tackles a business with a reputation for poor fundamental economics, it is the reputation of the business that remains intact.

If you combine ignorance and profit making, then you get some interesting results.

When you invest, you have to take some risk. The future is always uncertain. I think a group of these stocks will do very well for several years. Some of them may not do well, but as a group they should do well. I could end up owning them for several years.

Why don't you invest in companies which you like? As West has said, "It's fantastic to have excess of good things."

The need for extensive diversification arises only when the investors don't understand what they are doing.

With enough insider information and a million dollars, you can go bankrupt in a year.

Would you believe that a few decades back they were growing shrimps at Coke and exploring for oil at Gillette? Loss of focus is what worries Charlie and me, when we contemplate investing in businesses that in generally looks outstanding.

Writing a cheque separates conviction from conversation.

You are neither right nor wrong because the crowd disagrees with you.

You can have a full and rewarding life without ever thinking about goodwill and its amortisation. But students of investment and management should understand the nuances of the subject. My own thinking has changed drastically from 35 years ago, when I was taught to favour tangible assets and to shun businesses whose value depended largely upon economic goodwill. This bias caused me to make many important business mistakes of omission although relatively few of commission. Keynes identified my problem, 'The difficulty lies not in the new ideas but in escaping from the old ones.' My escape was long delayed, in part because most of what I had been taught by the same teacher had been (and continues to be) so extraordinarily valuable. Ultimately, business experience, direct and vicarious, produced my present strong preference for businesses that possess large amounts of enduring goodwill and that utilise a minimum of tangible assets.

You can't correctly invest unless you think independently. And the truth is you are neither right nor wrong because people agree with you. You're right because your facts and reasoning are right. In the end, that's what counts.

You do things when the opportunities come along. I've had periods in my life when I've had a bundle of ideas come along, and I've had long dry spells. If I get an idea next week, I'll do something. If not, I won't do a damn thing.

You don't have to think about everything. It was Isaac Newton who had said, "What others see in the world, I have seen more than that, because I am standing on the shoulders of a giant. There is nothing wrong in standing on others' shoulders."

You have to think about things that have never happened before. You always want to have plenty of money around.

You have to think for yourself. It always amazes me how people with high IQ, mindlessly imitate. I never get good ideas talking to other people.

You know it; you have heard people talking about it. You know it; there is uncertainty at all times. I mean, there was uncertainty in 2007, we did not know that it was uncertainty. There was uncertainty on 10 September, 2001.

You need to do very few things right, as long as you avoid big mistakes.

You should invest in a business that even a fool can run because someday a fool will.

Your goal as an investor should be simply to purchase at a rational price, and it should be easily understood in business that whose earnings are virtually certain to be materially higher, five, ten and twenty years from now. Over the time, you will find only a few companies that meet those standards. So when you see one that qualifies, you should buy a meaningful amount of stock.

Your premium brand must produce something special; otherwise it will not get business.

□

Timeline

Education

1947 – Woodrow Wilson High School, Washington D.C.

1947-48 – Wharton School, Pennsylvania.

1950 – B.Sc. degree from Nebraska University.

1951 – M.S. Degree in Economics from Columbia University.

Employment

1951-54 – Buffett-Falk and Company, Investment Salesman in Omaha.

1954-56 – Graham-Neumann Corporation, New York as Securities Analyst.

1956-69 – Buffett Partnership Limited, Omaha as General Partner.

1970 onwards – Berkshire Hathaway's Chairman and CEO.

Life

1943 – At the age of 13, Warren filed his first income tax return and claimed a rebate of $ 35 for his bicycle.

1945 – At the age of 15, while studying in the last year of his high school in partnership with his classmate he bought a used pinball machine for $ 25 and placed it in a barber's shop.

1949 – At the age of 19, when Warren was studying at Pennsylvania University's Wharton School, he joined the Alpha Sigma Phi fraternity. His father and uncle were also in the fraternity.

1950 – Warren applied for admission in Harvard Business School but his application was rejected as he was under age. Then he sought admission in Columbia Business School, because he knew that security analysts like Benjamin Graham and David Dodd were teaching there.

1951 – Twenty One year old Warren came to know that Benjamin Graham was the Chairman of G.I.E.C.O. Insurance Company in Washington. On one Saturday he boarded a train and reached Washington. He kept knocking at the headquarter door till he was allowed to enter. There he met the Vice-Chairman of the company Lotimer Davidson, who was not only extremely impressed by him, but they also became good friends. He discussed about the insurance business for 4 hours. Later Davidson recalled that within 15 minutes dialogue with Warren made him understood that he was an, 'extraordinary person.'

1952 – Twenty two year old Warren married Susan Thompson.

1953 – Twenty three year old Warren became father. His daughter was named Susan Alice Buffett.

1954 – Benjamin Graham offered him a job in his partnership company on an annual salary of $ 12,000. He worked there with Walter Schloss.

1956 – Warren's second child, a son Howard Graham Buffett was born. Benjamin Graham retired and he dissolved his partnership. Warren's personal savings increased to more than 140,000 dollars. Warren returned to Omaha and set up an investment partnership company named, 'Buffett Partnership.'

1957 – Warren has three partnership companies. Twenty-seven years old Warren buys a five bedroom stucco house on Farnam Street in Omaha for 31,500 dollars.

1958 – Twenty-eight years old Warren's third child a son, Peter Andrew Buffett is born. He has 5 partnership companies.

1959 – Warren has 6 partnership companies. He meets Charlie Munger.

1960 – Thirty year old Warren has 7 partnerships - Buffett Associates, Buffett Fund, Dacee, Emdee, Glenoff, Mo-Buff and Underwood, Dempster and Sanborn Map Company.

1961 – Warren's holding in Sanborn Map Company exceeds 35 per cent and he is appointed on its board.

1962 – Warren becomes a millionaire. In January 1962, the net worth of his partnerships was worth 7,178,500 dollars and Warren's share was worth 1,025,000 dollars. He started buying shares of Berkshire Hathaway.

1965 – Thirty-five year old Warren acquires control of Berkshire Hathaway and appoints a new CEO to run the textile business of the company.

1966 – Warren invests in a privately owned departmental store in Baltimore, Maryland, 'Hochchild-Kohn and Company.'

1969 – After his most successful year, Warren dissolved his partnerships and distributed the wealth to the partners. The wealth included shares of Berkshire Hathaway.

1970 – As the Chairman of Berkshire Hathaway, he started writing his annual letters to the shareholders, which became famous overtime.

1973 – Warren started buying shares of, 'Washington Post'. The company's owner Katharine Graham and Warren become close friends. Warren was appointed on the Board of Directors of the company.

1974 – S.E.C. starts investigating a merger done by Warren and Berkshire.

1977 – Berkshire buys, 'Buffalo Evening News' secretly for 325 million dollars. Berkshire started buying shares of ABC.

Berkshire's share started the year at the rate of 775 dollars per share and ended the year at 1310 dollars per share. Warren's holding was valued at 620 million dollars. (When Berkshire's share was quoting at 290 dollars per share, Warren's holding was valued at 140 million dollars). 'Forbes' magazine included his name in the list of the world's richest men for the first time.

1980 – Berkshire buys stock in RJ Reynolds (Tobacco), ALCOA (Metals and Mining), Pinkerton (Professional Services), Cleveland-Cliffs Iron (Metals and Mining), National Detroit (Banking), Times Mirror (Publishing) and National Student Marketing (Financial Services).

1981 – Berkshire buys Arcata (Forest products/Paper) and GATX (machinery).

1982 – Buffalo Evening News is the only local newspaper of Buffalo and its name is changed to Buffalo News. The newspaper earns $19 million in its first year without competition. By the late eighties, the Buffalo News is earning $40 million a year. Berkshire invests in Time (Publishing), Crum & Forster (Insurance).

1983 – Berkshire merges with Blue Chip Stamps, which was a majority owned subsidiary of Berkshire.

2001 – The acquisitions and purchases continue to increase. Berkshire acquires Johns Manville Corp (building products), MiTek, a provider of steel connector products, design engineering software and ancillary services for the global building components market. Berkshire goes on to acquire XTRA Corporation (transport containers), H&R Block (Financial Services) and Moody's Corporation (Financial Services). Insurance claims from the 9/11 terrorist attack total $2.28 billion. Buffett apologizes to his shareholders for failing to foresee the risk and properly price insurance coverage.

2002 – Warren entered into 11 billion dollars worth of forward contracts to sell American Dollars against other currencies. (After 4 years he earned a profit of more than 2 billion dollars on these contracts). Berkshire acquire Larson-Juhl, a custom picture frame maker, Fruit of the Loom (textile), Albecca (picture framing), Garan (apparel), CTB (farming equipment) and The Pampered Chef (kitchenware). Berkshire and other investment groups buy $500 million in bonds issued by Level 3 Communications, the former Omaha fiber network company.

2003 – Berkshire acquires McLane (wholesale distributor), Clayton Homes (housing) and Burlington Industries, one of the worlds's most diversified marketers and manufacturers of soft goods for apparel and interior furnishings.

2004 – Warren's wife Susie passes away. Bill Gates is elected as a Director for Berkshire Hathaway.

2005 – Berkshire acquires Medical Protective Company (Medical Malpractice Carrier) and Forest River (leisure vehicles). Despite insurance business losses of about $2.5 billion caused by Hurricane Katrina, Berkshire records a gain of $5.6 billion. Berkshire's subsidiary, Shaw Industries, buys stock in Honeywell International. Berkshire joins the fun by buying Procter and Gamble (Consumer Goods) and Anheuser-Busch (Food and Beverage). Berkshire stock crosses $90,000 per share.

2006 – Seventy-five year old Warren announces in June that he would donate 83 per cent of his share holding in Berkshire Hathaway, in instalments to 5 philanthropic organizations from July 2006. The largest donation would be Bill and Melinda Gates Foundation. Warren marries Astrid Menks.

The list of acquisitions and stock purchases continue – Business Wire (media distributor). Russell Corporation (athletic apparel). Eighty per cent of the Iscar Metalworking Companies (IMC) in a transaction that valued IMC at US$5 billion. Applied Underwriters (insurance). TTI Inc (electronic components distributor). Southern Energy Homes (utility). Brooke Sports (athletic apparel). Berkshire stock crosses $100,000 per share.

2007 – In a letter to shareholders, Buffett announces that he is looking for a young successor or perhaps successors to run Berkshire. Buffett had previously selected Lou Simpson, who manages the investment *via* G.E.I.C.O. to fill that role. However, Simpson is only six years younger than Buffett. The companies bought that year include– Boat America Corporation which owns Seaworthy Insurance Company and controls the Boat Owners Association of the United States. Leading jewellery manufacturers Bel-Oro International and Aurafin LLC, which merges into Richline Group. sixty per cent of Marmon Holdings (holding company that owns companies producing electrical components). SE Homes (home construction). BoatUS (Boat America Corporation is the main supplier of towing, insurance and other services to the non-profit boater's association).

2008 – 'Forbes' magazine names him the richest man in the world. Before this, Bill Gates held this distinction for the last 13 years. Berkshire buys out Marmon Holdings and Coachmen Industries becomes a part of Forest River (leisure vehicles). Berkshire buys $4.4b in bonds from Mars Inc (food and beverage). Makes $680m in profit from the investment.

2009 – Berkshire's subsidiary, Shaw Industries, acquires Sportexe (a leading synthetic turf company). Berkshire acquires Cavalier Homes (home building company). A $5 billion "paper", loss on investments and derivatives triggers a first-quarter loss for Berkshire. It is the biggest loss since the 9/11 terrorist attack. But earnings rebound later in the year.

2010 – Berkshire buys out railroad company Burlington Northern for $44 billion. As a result of the acquisition, Berkshire enters the S&P 500, replacing Burlington Northern Santa Fe. Berkshire subsidiary, McLane Company, acquires Kahn Ventures. Berkshire invests in Munich Re (Insurance).

2011 – Berkshire acquires Lubrizol (Specialty Chemicals).

2012 – Berkshire acquires Omaha World-Herald (Publishing) and invests in IBM (Technology).

2013 – Berkshire acquires a 50% stake in H. J. Heinz Company (Food and Beverage).

2014 and Beyond – As Berkshire continues to accumulate more cash, it's capital spending will increase and you will no doubt see big deals occur going forward. Buffett has one of the most illustrious investing careers the world has ever seen.

The story is not over yet.

□□□